I did it
the hard way

I did it the hard way

Tommy Smith

Arthur Barker Limited London
A subsidiary of Weidenfeld (Publishers) Limited

Published in Great Britain by Arthur Barker Limited
91 Clapham High Street, London SW4 7TA

ISBN 0 213 16766 2

Printed and bound in Great Britain by
Morrison & Gibb Ltd, London and Edinburgh

Contents

Acknowledgements

My thanks go to David Stuckey for helping me get it all together, and to those who tried to make sense of the tapes we made, and to all my friends and people whom I haven't managed to mention but who kept reminding me to give them one – cheers!

T.S.

The photographs in the book are reproduced by kind permission of the following:

Central Press no. 12
Liverpool Daily Post and Echo nos 13 (Eddie Barford), 14, 15 and 17 (John Davidson)
Liverpool Weekly News no. 7
London News Service no. 20
Harry Ormisher back cover and nos 9 and 10
Press Association no. 18
Stephen Shakeshaft front cover and nos 16, 21, 22, 23 and 24
Tommy Smith nos 1, 2, 4 and 5
Sun Newspapers no. 3
Syndication International nos 6 and 11 (A. Markey)

For Sue, Darren and Janette,
my mother and Sue's family

1 The Glory that was Rome

They say all roads lead to Rome – ours had begun in 1977 at Setubal in Spain, but my personal road to Rome started some thirty years or more before, when as a lad I used to kick a ball around the terraced streets not far from Anfield, in Liverpool, where I was born and brought up.

I knew I could play football even before I went to school, and this love for the game led me to play in any spare time I had. I used to find time for maybe three or four games a week in various boys' leagues or friendly kick-arounds.

My enthusiasm for the game also led me to become captain of a number of Liverpool schools and junior sides, and eventually to captain the England Under-23s, and then Liverpool FC, whom I joined as a groundstaff lad of fifteen.

I have had a long and full football career – I have won most of the honours the game could give, and from rough and ready beginnings have played all over the world for my country and my club. I have been a part of the great Liverpool side of the 1960s, savouring the thrill of winning the FA Cup for the first time in the club's history, when we beat Leeds in 1965, and then the same year sharing the heartache of being deprived of European glory in a shameful showdown with Inter-Milan. I have been captain of the 1970s side which brought the first of our European trophies to Anfield – the UEFA Cup in 1973, when we beat Moenchengladbach – and that same year we were also League champions.

It was a tremendous double to achieve with the relatively new and exciting team that Bill Shankly had moulded, and after that season winning seemed to come naturally to us. There was always something at the end of the rainbow – the FA Cup the following year, the UEFA Cup and League champions again in 1976.

In 1977, as the season progressed, it began to dawn on people that we were in with a very real chance of gaining this quite fantastic treble – League champions, FA Cup winners and maybe European Cup winners, too.

Personally, I was convinced that the 1977 season would mark the twilight of my playing days. I'd had an op for a Baker's cyst on the back of my leg that Christmas, there had been talk of me taking over as player-manager of Wigan Athletic (that was before they were elected to the League), I was thinking of going back to America, and plans were laid for my testimonial. So I was going to pack it in, and if I was keeping myself fit after coming out of hospital, it wasn't so much to see the English season out as to make sure I was in good shape for a summer in the States.

Then suddenly I was in the thick of this tremendous campaign – two cup runs, a gripping League programme . . . everything seemed to be happening at once. I had been playing football all my life, but I'd never experienced a build-up like those few months leading up to Rome.

The lads were marvellous. I think being used to success meant we didn't allow ourselves to get worked up. We seemed to be taking everything in our stride, nice and relaxed, which was good. The reporters who swarmed around us seemed more on edge than we were.

I don't think we allowed ourselves to think about the treble until we were down to those last vital games of the season. We clinched the League and then we set off for Wembley to play Manchester United in the FA Cup final.

I suppose if we admitted to any nerves at all it was over that Wembley date with United. And as it turned out it wasn't to be our day. I still don't think we deserved to get beaten and it gives me some satisfaction to know it will always be remembered as the final Liverpool lost, and not the final United won.

We were all a bit choked after the game. We had done some advertising for a menswear firm and they'd given us these outfits to wear at Wembley – blue jackets with grey flannels. But footballers are a superstitious lot, and Emlyn Hughes turned up as he usually liked to in his favourite old suit.

Sitting around in the dressing-room afterwards, Joe Fagan tried to lift our depression, and I said to him: 'Well, one good thing's come out of this game. Emlyn can go and burn that scruffy suit and come looking smart for a change!'

But the fact remained – the treble was lost. If any English club was going to do the treble, it had to be Liverpool – I can't see anybody else getting that close ever again.

Looking back on Wembley, Bob Paisley took a bit of stick for not playing Ian Callaghan from the start. People said he should have stuck Cally in the hole, as we say, and let everybody else sort themselves out. It might have been a different game then; as it was, Cally came on late in the match, but it was really too late to make any difference.

You could say, though, that Manchester United did us a great favour by winning at Wembley, for it meant we went to Rome the following Wednesday for the European Cup final in a much more relaxed state of mind. The pressures had gone, the treble was lost, and we were determined to enjoy ourselves – not only to make up for losing at Wembley but also to avenge the memories of ten years previously, when we had lost that dreadful semi-final tie with Inter-Milan. That still remains the cruellest moment of my football career – Liverpool FC have had the longest continuous run in European competitions of any English club, and we could and should have reached the European final in 1965.

But we had used the intervening years well, and fancied our chances in Rome because we'd learnt to play as a European side, where the quickest way forward is often to push the ball back and frustrate your opponents into making mistakes.

It makes a difference, playing abroad. I remember we were in the Cup Winners' Cup final at Hampden Park in 1966 against Borussia Dortmund and we didn't play it like a European game. We were at home, if you like, and expected to win. We weren't mentally prepared to play it in a European way – and we lost.

That's probably why, the year after Rome, when we played Bruges in the European Cup final at Wembley, it was more of a bore. It lacked the continental atmosphere. It makes a great difference, playing on foreign soil.

As I said, our road to Rome that year had begun against Setubal and I was on the bench over in Spain, even though I played in the return leg at Anfield. We won both these games quite comfortably, and then we had to play the French champions, St Etienne, in the quarter-finals. Again I was on the bench over there when we were beaten 1–0, but I played at Anfield when we beat them 3–1. That was the night Davey Fairclough scored a fantastic goal.

Next came the European semis, and by then Phil Thompson had got himself injured, so I found myself first choice for the side against Zurich. Actually I slipped up and gave a penalty away in the opening minutes. Their outside left was a bit tricky, and I'd fouled him once. The second time we clashed I didn't foul him, but the way he dived it looked bad. It was just one of those things, and they went one up. In the end, though, we murdered them 3–1, and it could have been six. When they came to Anfield for the second leg we coasted through with another three goals.

Now for the final in Rome; a lot of people were saying Moenchengladbach were due for a win against us, because we'd beaten them in the UEFA Cup final a few years before. They had one or two fine players like Bonhoff and Bertie Vogts, who was a world-class defender and whom they reckoned could take care of Keegan. But the bookies weren't soft – they still made Liverpool FC favourites.

I remember talking to Denis Law outside our hotel the night before the game and he said it would be a tough final, because the Germans were showing that extra bit of flair. But we'd had spies round to see them train and I said I reckoned we could beat them in the air, because they looked shaky on crosses.

Continental players seem to be very good at ball control, clipping good passes and that, but few of them seem to know what goes on in the air, how to play with their heads.

So Denis and I were talking and saying they appeared to be struggling a wee bit in the air in the penalty box, and wasn't it a shame John Toshack wasn't playing for us now. When we'd played Moenchengladbach before, Tosh had been involved in three aerial goals we'd scored – two direct from headers and one nodded down for Keegan to blast in.

In practice games that season Kevin and myself had worked on going up for Steve Heighway's corners, with me coming off opposing players and flicking the ball on to cause havoc in the opponents' penalty area and hoping maybe Kevin would slot one or two goals in. But we'd never practised where I'd be in a position to head for goal. . . .

Anyway, came the final in that magnificent Italian stadium, which seemed to be alive with Liverpool fans. We scored first through Terry McDermott, through patience more than anything else – we slowed the game down, pushed the ball around, kept possession, tried to run them off their feet.

It was a warm night and I remember thinking at half-time that things seemed to be working like magic. But I also knew (we all did) that Moenchengladbach either had to come at us soon or get beat by six goals.

So when the second half started it was no surprise when they went off quick, really full force. Jimmy Case tried to lay a ball back to me, mistimed it, and their little winger pounced on it and belted it past Ray Clemence. It was, truthfully, a terrific goal.

We suddenly started going a bit erratic and they had a couple of chances to put themselves 2–1 up. Clem kept us in the game with two very good saves, but for ten or fifteen minutes it could have gone either way. Then we got this corner. . . .

I was in the penalty box with Kevin and we had a word or two, mapping out what we might do – not a full board meeting or anything, because we both knew what we had to do, more or less.

Anyway, Steve Heighway drove this ball over – it's got to be the greatest cross I've ever seen, and at a perfect height. There's this German fellow between Kevin and me, not knowing whether to wait for Keegan to make a move or go with me – in the end their defence left me so much room it was untrue.

I'm not the fastest person in the world but I can steal a yard on anyone, and they just seemed to stand there like they were frozen, including the goalkeeper. So I went up and met the ball with my head, and as soon as I hit it I knew it was on target, but I still had visions of their giant goalkeeper plucking it out of the air.

Next thing is – he's picking it out of the back of the net! That just has to be the greatest feeling I've ever had in my whole life. I can count the number of goals I've scored with my head on the fingers of one hand and I've certainly never caught one like that – I tell you, it looks better every time I see it!

Incidentally, the first time I did see it was in Hong Kong of all places. I had gone away a week or so after the final on tour with Bobby Charlton's XI and one night in the hotel I sat down and saw the whole recording through on television. You can imagine how excitable a Chinese commentator can get describing a goal!

That goal was the straw that seemed to break Moenchengladbach. The rest of the game was a bit of an anti-climax. We settled down and started pushing the ball around more confidently, creating a few chances. Then Kevin got away with the ball, and Bertie Vogts, who'd been chasing him all evening, caught up with him just inside the box and brought him down. So it was left to Phil Neal to finish it off with a penalty.

Well then, it all started after the match, all this Roy of the Rovers business, because as far as most people knew – and as far as I knew – it might have been my last game for Liverpool. I don't think it all sank in until I got home.

Even today, people I meet in the street say, 'Hello, Tommy lad! All right?' And they nod their head as if to head a ball. I can understand folk doing that if they had passed Dixie Dean in the street, but me! I can remember scoring a header when I was a kid in a Reds *v.* Whites pre-season trial; I scored one against Everton, a diving header that went between Gordon West's legs, and I scored one the season after the European Cup against Leicester. That, I think, is all.

But it was a dream of a moment, even if it does still bug me to be introduced as 'Tommy Smith – you know, the lad who scored that header in the European Cup final in Rome. . . .' I played for Liverpool since I was a kid of seventeen, won a couple of FA Cup winners' medals, four league title medals, a couple of UEFA Cup medals, played for England . . . I'd like to be remembered for more than just one goal!

2 Schooldays

I was born in 1945 by the ground, by Anfield. And as a lad I used to play football in the streets – and break a few windows. It was all part of growing up.

In fact, looking back on it, I can't remember a time when I didn't play football. The houses all had little bay windows that fronted the pavements and the streets were on a slope, so I used to tap the ball against each bay, doing a one-two going up the hill. It was harder coming down because the ball would run away from you.

As a kid I can vaguely remember moving to a street called Buckingham Street, off Great Homer Street, where there was a chap with a horse and cart who used to deliver coal. We lived in the flat above his coal yard.

We left there when I was maybe four or five and went to live in Lambeth Road, at no. 9 in the lower part, the Sandhills end. I couldn't play football in Lambeth Road because it was pretty busy, so I used to play in the street next but one, which was Elstow Street, where we had relatives.

My dad, Matty, worked on the fruit at the docks all his life. He started off driving a wagon dock to dock, mostly Preston, but later he became a foreman and used to drive home in a little van.

My mum, Margaret, is Irish by descent – Meehan was my grandfather's name – and she's the little goer of the family. Dad was a big lad, and nobody told him off – except her.

She was the guiding influence on the marriage – if there was any saving-up to be done for Christmas or holidays she'd do it. Dad was probably a little too easy-going, but his heart was always in the right place.

I remember getting copped one day, playing football on Commercial Road – which was a main thoroughfare – by a policeman who took me round to our house and said he'd have to report it. Dad thought nothing more of it till about two days later when a sergeant came round. 'I hear your son's been playing football in the main road,' he said.

Now my dad, whom I respected a lot – I mean, he was never that strict but he always made sense – had a quick think, and in his crafty way he said, 'Oh aye, I've been telling him not to play out there, but he threatened to come down and see you, and report me for hitting him!'

That threw the sergeant a bit. He replied, 'Yes, well, there's a lot of that going on. Don't you worry about it. If he comes down to see me, I'll clip his ear and send him back, and then you can give him another clout. . . .'

So my dad got me out of that one great. And I was looking at him all the time, but saying nothing. He used his head that time – magic!

Dad worked for a firm called May Harrison for over twenty years until they folded, then he was offered a job with the Mersey Docks and Harbour Board. He never drank that much, and he was a big fellow – I guess he was about seventeen stone – and coming off the docks the lads used to go for a pint, but he wasn't that particular about it. One night, though, I think he did have a few and came home late, and my mum had murder with him. So rather than mess us around, he packed the Mersey Docks job in and went to work for a firm in St Helens as a foreman.

On the docks they have different signs on the crates for different foods from different countries, and because he'd done it for so long he knew them all. If there was anything coming off that had a sign on it, he could tell . . . 'That's apples,' 'That goes there, like.' It seems he was quite good at it, so eventually he got a foreman's job.

We lived in a little terraced house and Dad would now and again get his finger out and do a bit of paper-hanging, but mostly Mum would do it, because he was such a heavy lad. Or she would come and ask me – I enjoyed it really. She never forced me to do anything I didn't want to.

And there was never any shortage of anything; at Christmas there was always fruit, and Mum used to work in a shop – a little fruit shop, as it happens.

I was an only child, but Dad had a couple of brothers and sisters and they'd come to visit us. He'd probably show more affection to my cousins than he did to me, perhaps because I was a boy and they were mostly girls. But Dad was always fair to me – he probably didn't think I'd mind him being nice to the girls, me being his lad and all.

The house had a front parlour, a middle room and a back kitchen. We used to live in the middle room – which was just as well. One day I remember a helluva bang and a lorry had embedded itself in our bay window. It didn't happen too often, but it did happen down Lambeth Road. Ours wasn't the only house to be hit like this. On a winter's day, with ice on the road, it'd be just like the dodgems out there.

I lived a bus ride away from Cardinal Godfrey School and living at the bottom of the road was a bit of luck because some mornings if I was late and knew the conductor, I could skip on the bus as it was climbing the hill.

Mind you, if I didn't know the conductor I'd have to race the bus up the road, and hope the lights were on red, so I had time to make it across Stanley Road to the bus-stop.

Mum's still alive, and in her sixties. One time I was doing an article for the *Liverpool Echo* and referred, without thinking, to 'the old lady'. Did I get into trouble over that! 'I'm your mother. I'm not your old lady.' She didn't consider it a term of affection. She's still the boss after all.

Dad died while I was still at school when he was only forty-four. A couple of years previously he'd got bitten by a spider while unloading boxes of bananas and became very ill. For a while it was touch and go, but he pulled through. This time he got a cold and after what he'd been through nobody thought anything of it. But it turned to double pneumonia. He was such a chubby lad and a big strong fellow, people thought, 'He'll get over it.' His death took everyone by surprise because we just didn't expect it.

I remember getting off a no. 46 bus at Everton Valley after a spot of training up Penny Lane and a cousin of mine, Pat Leary, was waiting for me. I thought, 'What the hell's going on?' I knew my dad was ill, and I'd been to see him in hospital, but I never suspected he was just going to keel over. Anyway she started crying and told me the news, and I didn't know what to do. Things changed overnight for me. . . .

School was a funny place. First of all I went to St John's Roman Catholic, then when I took the eleven-plus I went to Archbishop (now Cardinal) Godfrey School, which grew out of the old St Mary's School in Breck Road, at the back of the picture house.

It's a great coincidence that these days my son Darren goes to St Mary's School in Crosby, which uses the same Christian brothers of St Mary who taught me.

Cardinal Godfrey School was only about four or five years old when I got there, and really concerned with getting into sport. They knew the only way they were going to be accepted on Merseyside, being a fairly new school, was to get involved in sport – any honours you got in education seemed to come after any honours you gained on the sports field. At least that was the impression I got. If you left school and went to university, fine – you got the praise eventually – but for instant success, football was the thing.

They tried introducing rugby into Cardinal Godfrey while I was there, but it never went. If you ever did anything wrong during lessons they used to say, 'Right, you're gonna play in the rugby team on Saturday' – that's how bad it was.

The first thing I noticed when I got to Cardinal Godfrey was that the juniors didn't play football; only the intermediates, the thirteen-year-olds. That didn't matter to me much because I'd joined the Lee Jones Boys Club in Scotland Road and used to play for them on Saturdays, but the teachers must have thought I was turning into a decent player, because I had been at the school no more than a year and was only just twelve when I was playing for the intermediates. The following year I was captain, with the additional responsibility of being in charge of the travelling arrangements for the school team.

The headmaster was a fellow called Brother Moran, and we used to call him Pop, a great old character, if a bit unpredictable. He used to carry a little stick under his gown, and you'd be walking along the corridor talking to him when all of a sudden – whack – he'd hit you. You'd look at him and ask, 'What was that for, sir?' and he'd say, 'We've just passed a sweet paper on the floor. You should have picked it up and put it in the bin!'

Anyway, he used to have me in his office – 'Sit down, have a cup of tea' – and give out the bus tickets for the away games. He'd get the bus manual out and he'd be working out which player went from where and what bus he'd have to catch, and even if you told him you only had to walk a hundred yards to get there he wouldn't have it and you'd end up with about six buses to catch.

Being crafty, I usually ended up with more tickets than Soft Joe . . . I'd end up going all the way to school on these tickets myself.

The first time I got into trouble at school was soon after I came from St John's. I didn't exactly get away with murder there but I was a big lad and nobody seemed to pick on me. Going to a new school, though, you got people coming in from down the south end, Scottie Road, Bootle and all over, all trying to prove themselves. It's a bit like a war game till you get settled.

Anyway there was this lad called Fatty Campbell and he was friends with another lad called Ossie, who came from down the Dingle. It was time to go home one day and I was picking up my books when Fatty spat at Ossie, missed him and hit me.

So I was over the desk and I butted him. He was bigger than me, but he still took a step back. There he was, scrambling along the floor, when who should come in but our teacher Tom Burke. He used to take us for sports and he knew I was a footballer, so he asked me what had happened. I said, in my best college accent, 'He spat at me, sir.'

Then he turned to Campbell and said, 'What happened?' and Campbell said, 'He butted me, sir.'

Tom Burke sized up the situation and turned to me and said: 'Let's put it this way, Smithy. He spat at you and I know you, coming from Scottie Road, couldn't do anything else but butt him back. . . .' I thought, I'm in for a right rollicking here. Then he turned to Campbell and said, 'Spitting's not nice, you know. If I ever catch you spitting again, I'll butt you and all! That's a terrible habit, that!' So Fatty got the worst of it.

Mr McEnery, who used to take us for English, had a terrible habit – he used to splutter and splatter his words about. The joke was if you sat in the front row you needed an umbrella. But nobody said anything to him because we were all terrified of him. The first time he took us he said, 'Right, if you do anything wrong in my lessons, which would you prefer – detention or the stick? Take a vote on it.' We thought, we'll get it over with quickly and we'll vote for the stick. So we did – and then he said, 'Right, if you do anything wrong . . . detention it is.' You know, he was one of those.

It was in one of his lessons that I got caught out one day. I was gazing out of the window, probably dreaming about the coming Saturday's match when I heard him call out my name: 'What's the answer, Smith!'

Now I didn't even know what the question was, so I had to admit I didn't know, and he came over and said: 'Pay attention, Smithy. Don't daydream about football all the time. Honestly, lad, the day you make a professional footballer, I'm going to go out and get myself roaring drunk.'

Well, many years later, having signed for Liverpool, done my groundstaff apprenticeship, proved my worth through the C team, the B team, the A team, the reserves and then the first team, picking up a few England Under-23 caps, an FA Cup-winner's medal and a League championship medal on the way, I made a return trip to my old school. Tucked under my arm was a bottle of whisky, a present for Mr McEnery.

We also had a tall, gangly Irishman who always called me 'Schmitt'. One time after he'd had a go at me he called me 'Schmitty' so I got up and in my best posh voice said, 'Excuse me, sir, my name's Smith, not Schmitt,' and I spelt it out for him.

That did it – he got really mad and came down to take a swipe at me, but he missed and smashed his wrist against the heavy central-heating pipes on the wall behind my head. Suddenly his watch went pop and broke into a hundred pieces. All the class was convulsed on the floor, and he lost control. . . . Magic really, times like that at school.

There was another fellow at St John's who was Polish and used to take us for French, which was useless because you could never really understand his English. We had another teacher, called Paddy Moore, who took us for maths, and we all used to get on well with him. He was big and muscular, and loved boxing. Sometimes, instead of maths he'd take us up the gym and give us a boxing lesson instead. One day he put me in the ring with a pal of mine called John McEvoy, and I swung one and hit him on the chin. He went down like a sack of muck and hit his head, so that was the end of the boxing lessons. But Paddy was crafty too – on holy days of obligation, we'd go to church on West Derby Road, and as we turned right on the way to the service he'd turn left and nip in the pub. Then as we filed back to school he'd nip out again and join us.

Actually I didn't mind maths, history, geography, that sort of thing. But I could never get on with English. My writing is still a scrawl and a letter of mine looks like a spider's. And I can't spell. I'm the worst speller in the world, but I don't mind drawing. I think that's where my interest in architecture started; later I had a hand in designing my own home. I used to like woodwork and metalwork, too; I was always good with my hands. But I didn't like the chemistry bit, or French.

Being a Roman Catholic school, religion played a large part in our school life. Pop Moran even tried to turn me off football at Anfield – Catholics were traditionally Everton supporters and players, Liverpool were the Protestant team. Pop honestly thought that being a Catholic I wouldn't be happy at Anfield.

But the distinction was never firm, even then. Perhaps twenty years before you wouldn't have found a Protestant playing for Everton, like you wouldn't have found a Protestant playing for Celtic. But now it doesn't matter, and even when I started playing it didn't mean that much.

I used to go to church – to St John's or St Alphonsus. But I remember when Dad died I took great exception to the parish priest drinking at the funeral. I was crying my eyes out, and so was Mum, and I got to thinking, 'There he is – he's supposed to be comforting us. Why's he hitting the bottle?'

I was at an age where I was starting to grow up and question these sort of things. And I was beginning to get fed up with people stuffing religion down my throat. I can well remember going to Friday afternoon benediction at St John's, and Friday mornings was the time you took your comics and your games to junior school. Church was compulsory on Friday afternoon, so you'd be sitting there with your comics on your lap. With kids of that age your mind's going to wander during the service; its only natural.

But I can remember one particular priest storming out of the pulpit regularly, and throwing the comics into the aisles and belting us round the ear – he was a real tyrant and we were only six or seven at the time.

I suppose I was always brought up a Catholic based on fear. On Friday evenings there used to be a row of four confessionals and you'd always try and pick the quiet priests. But there'd always be one who would insist on talking loudly – 'Speak up lad, I can't hear. . . .' – and there'd be queues for the other three but his would be empty.

If you can centre your life around religion, then that's great. Probably I've been too busy, and what I saw as a kid put me off to a certain extent. I certainly haven't stuffed religion down my children's throats, but they know the difference between right and wrong.

I'm not against religion, but I've never found it that comforting. Maybe one day I will. . . .

There's no doubt about it – I played an awful lot of football while I was at school. On Saturdays I'd play for Cardinal Godfrey in the morning and Lee Jones Boys Club in the afternoon. Then during the week I'd play for Liverpool Juniors or

Liverpool Schoolboys – it all got a bit involved – and we'd play of an evening. So maybe I was playing three or four games a week.

I was captain of Liverpool Juniors and later became captain of the Schoolboy Seniors. I was only fourteen then and if you were captain you were also cock of the class at school. You would be monitor and when the teacher left the room you'd be the one to take care of everything that went on.

The teacher would say, 'Now, Smith, use your head, because if anyone starts yelling, you'll be in trouble as well.' So I used to make sure the kids knew the score. I used to protect them, if you like; if ever there was a confrontation or if anyone needed belting they'd come and ask me to do it. I was never a bully, but it was just one of the responsibilities you took on as cock of the class, that's the way it worked. And the kids always knew that if the teacher belted me for not keeping order, I'd certainly belt them for landing me in it.

Before I got to Cardinal Godfrey I'd played football at Anfield. While I was at St John's, we played St Christopher's in the semis of the Junior Cup and drew with them at Long Lane 3–3, then we went to play at Jericho Farm and drew again, one apiece – and they missed a penalty. Finally we met them at Melwood, Liverpool FC's training ground, and beat them 1–0. On account of that the organizers said, 'Right, you can play at Anfield.'

They bought us new kit – it was like a Celtic kit – and although we played on the full-size pitch they lowered the crossbars for us, because you can imagine ten- or eleven-year-olds in goal! You're not talking about these days when you get strapping six-footers at twelve or thirteen. We were only kids, and looked it.

We played a team from down Scottie Road – I can never remember their name, probably because we got beat 3–2, and I was playing right-back then. That was actually the first Liverpool Junior Cup, and I've still got my losers' medal.

Then when I started playing for Cardinal Godfrey they had some really good players, and one year within a week we got to three finals. On the Monday we met St Theresa's, Chris Lawler was in their side, and we beat them 6–1. I scored two – my first goals at Anfield, and I was only fourteen at the time. Then on the Wednesday we met my old school St John's in the Catholic Leagues final – they'd won their league and we'd won ours. Before we went out against St John's I remember Tom Burke saying to us, 'Let's have a few goals,' and by half-time we were three up. At half-time he gave us our tactic talk: 'If they score, you score . . . simple as that.' It was that sort of game.

Anyway, they scored, so we scored, then they scored again, but by then it was all over – and we ran out winners 4–2.

St Theresa's and Cardinal Godfrey were really the top two sides, though, and we met them again on the Saturday in the third final, and beat them again 2–1. So suddenly I went from one losers' medal to three winners' medals, having swapped my position to centre-forward and scored four out of the twelve goals.

When playing for St John's, we had to go and collect the goal-posts and take them to Walton Hall Park, and it was usually arranged that the forwards took them there and the defence humped them back. So being a bit crafty and one of the bigger lads, I'd start the game at centre-half and switch to centre-forward at half-time; then there'd be an argument as to why I didn't carry the posts . . . you had to hump them a good two miles as well. They were heavy things for little lads.

At Cardinal Godfrey's ground at Cantril Farm we at least had proper permanent goal-posts and they even put nets up, which wasn't bad. There were proper showers in the dressing-rooms, too, which meant you didn't have to scrub the mud off in a bucket of cold water, or go home stinking.

There used to be trouble sometimes. I remember one time we played St Philhelmena's and beat them 6–1 on their own ground, and they got a bit mad about it. We stuck together on the walk home, but suddenly a gang of them went for us. We managed to cop a bus and get away but some of our lads got beaten up. A week or so later we had the police down making inquiries about it.

We played St Philly's again in the semi-finals of one of the cups at Melwood and beat them 8–2, really battered them. But that time there were plenty of teachers around to see there was no trouble.

I always thought I could play football but there was something there to stop me getting too cocky about it and keep my feet on the ground. I remember once playing against St Christopher's for Cardinal Godfrey and a lad named Tony Lamb was on our side. I'd been playing wing-half and was having the easiest of jobs clipping the ball through their defence for him to run on to it and put it in the back of the net. One time I turned round, all big-headed, and said, 'Nice ball, eh, Lammy?' And he said, 'Oh, you never meant it . . .'

Another time, when I was captain of Lancashire Schoolboys, playing centre-half, we played at Shrewsbury and got beaten 3–2. It was during that game that our goalkeeper got carried off. We put somebody else in goal, but I hadn't organized it properly to hold what advantage we had – we might have won if we hadn't continued playing as if we had eleven men on the field. And I got stick afterwards for not seeing to that – it was a good lesson in captaincy, if you like, but it was hard-learnt.

I also used to play for another side down Scottie Road when I played for Lee Jones Boys Club. We used to have street games – somebody would organize a street team and we used to play on Sundays in a street league knock-out competition. I remember we even got to the final of that.

Between the time I was fourteen and sixteen there was an awful lot going on. Within two years I played for maybe ten or eleven teams at odd times.

3 Anfield's Where the Action is

When my dad died I didn't know what I was going to do. I was playing soccer for Liverpool Schoolboys and had already had offers from Liverpool. I had dreams of being an architect, too, and I wanted to go to night school and study.

I always knew I had a bit of a football brain. We used to play house games at school – I was in Downey House, and we had one or two who didn't want to play football. They'd rather wander off and play tag or something. I had a go at some of them one day. They said, 'We're no budding Billy Liddell's.' I said, 'You don't have to be Donald Ducks either.' I could never understand why they weren't interested in the game – I was always interested and felt I could do something in it.

Dad never admitted to taking a pride in me playing football, but if ever there was a pair of boots or anything to be bought he would get them. He never complained because I was playing a lot, just so long as I did the things I was supposed to do around the house – tidying up, lighting the fire, bits and bats like that – but as soon as I neglected anything that's when he'd have a go.

I respected him a lot. You could have an argument with him, but he was always fair.

As I say, when he died it was obvious I had to make a decision about my future. In the end Tosh Moore, the Anfield scout, came down to the house and had a chat with Mum. Tosh was a great old character, and a chain-smoker – he'd light one, then another, then another . . . go through maybe a hundred a day. He persuaded Mum there'd be no trouble about my joining the groundstaff at Liverpool FC.

But the problem was, once you got a scholarship to go to college you couldn't get out of it. You had to pay some gratuity or something to the Education Committee . . . one of those stupid things.

Finally I remember going down Sir Thomas Street with Mum and going in to see the Education Committee; they came up with a grant of a pound a week to keep me at school.

Well, you're talking about a 5 ft 8 ins, eleven-stone lad. I'd eat more than a pound's worth of food a day, let alone a week.

So we went back to Liverpool FC to see Bill Shankly and he said, 'No problems. We'll sort it out.' Their offer was £7 a week – no messing. So that was that.

Bill Shankly had joined Liverpool late in 1959 and it was around Easter 1960 when I first went to see him. I had a fortnight's holiday owing me and I remember when I joined the groundstaff before the start of the 1960–61 season I got paid £14 to compensate for that holiday (£10 after tax) and I was over the moon!

I'd already tasted a bit of glory, if you like, and had been tried out in various positions on the field. When I played for Lancashire Schoolboys, Tommy Wright, who went on to become an Everton full-back, played with me. But in those days I was moved up from centre-half to inside-left and Tommy was always inside-right, to see if we could get some goals. We finished up with seventeen apiece for the Schoolboys.

When we played Durham Schoolboys at Goodison I was even switched to centre-forward and scored three, and Tommy scored one. We trounced them 6–2, and when we played Cheshire Schoolboys at Old Trafford I got one that day, too.

They'd had England Schoolboys trials previous to this at Barnsley and I was one of the subs who came on in the second half. Someone gave me a kick so I had to go off again. I think I played about twenty minutes and that was the sum total of my first England trial! But they had one or two good players on the field. One outstanding lad was David Pleat, who eventually became manager of Luton. I came across him again when I played for the England Youth side.

I think the chances of getting a trial if you were a northerner were twice as hard than if you were from the south, but anyway I wasn't really interested. I just wanted to get the season over and join Liverpool.

The first year I joined Liverpool I also played for a team called Liverpool County – they used to pick a team from Liverpool, Everton, Tranmere and one or two others. We ended up going to Ireland and playing an Irish League side and winning 6–2.

I scored three that day and it was the first time I got a laugh out of journalists – it was the first time I'd got my name in print for doing something special on the football field, and they called me 'Fred Smith' – typical Irish humour! But the English papers were no better – one of the Sundays quoting Bill Shankly on his future stars had him saying, 'I've got this local lad who's going to be good – Jimmy Smith . . .' You can't win.

The second time I went to Ireland was my first trip abroad with Liverpool FC and it was useful, because I was still only sixteen, to be there with the pros and see how they relaxed, how they reacted; was like learning a trade right from the start.

Liverpool first of all arranged for me to train as an amateur on Tuesday and Thursday nights and maybe stay at school and pass some exams to become an architect. But when Dad died things got a bit awkward, so with Tosh Moore's guidance we went to see Shanks, having made sure I could leave school. Shanks was very keen, because as well as myself he signed Phil Tinney, Georgie Scott and Hamish McKenzie as schoolboys at the same time – we were his first signings.

The first impressions I gained of Bill Shankly were nothing special. He was just this Scots fellow who'd taken over at Liverpool. He hadn't been in the job long enough for people to start talking about him, or even know him – and all I wanted to do was play football. To me, here was this little Scots fellow eager for me to do just that, and it suited me down to the ground.

When I was a schoolkid I just thought about football and about playing as a way of getting out of school. And when I joined Liverpool FC as a groundstaff lad, I thought it was going to be so glamourous. I really got kidded. . . .

Anfield had always been a shrine for me and to go there felt good – but, truthfully, it looked as though it was falling down. I remember thinking it could do with a good coat of paint – little knowing I'd be doing it myself in four weeks' time. It was so run-down that to see it now is quite unbelievable. Shanks put so much of himself into that ground. Personally I didn't go there to paint the place or clean out the toilets – I went to play football. So the first day when I turned up for work and they gave me a fork to go out and fork over the pitch, I couldn't believe it!

The season had just finished and we had to get stuck in. There were about ten of us taken on at that time, and we all mucked in together, so they could sow the new grass seed.

I'd had all the visions of football clubs as illustrious places where everything is gleaming and shining, and all you do all day is play football. I was so put off it was untrue.

They would string the ground off in a diamond shape from the penalty area to the half-way line – that's the piece of the park where most of the action is after all – and all of us, plus the maintenance men, painters, anybody, would get stuck in and fork the pitch. Then the groundsman, Arthur Riley, would follow us round and sow the seed. We'd do it as early and as quickly as possible so it would have the maximum time to grow. And after we'd done the main playing area we'd come back and do the corners. While all this was going on, another couple of lads would be sifting topsoil in a big sifter over by the main stand. We did this for a good two weeks or so, and in between were sent off to make the tea.

Before the season came up we'd be painting the toilets, painting the stands – I mean standing up in the main stand maybe twenty or thirty feet up, and I'm not the bravest of men when it comes to heights. We'd also paint Melwood and Shanks's house. Any manual job that needed doing, we'd tackle it. I can remember Bob Paisley – he was first-team trainer then – saying, 'Come on, you look a big strong lad. Give me a hand.'

And we ended up going under the Kop roof and cutting out a girder that one of the stilemen had said was in his way. Bob redirected it and we cemented another one in. He also had us making new dug-outs, reorganizing the bandbox and the system for putting up the half-time scores – the old slots to take the numbers had gone rusty.

Joe Fagan, the reserve-team trainer, and Reuben Bennett, the head trainer – we all used to muck in, and we all felt a part of something special. But then that was the makings of the club.

The only time I got to see a football was on Friday mornings when we'd play against the binmen in the car-park, having some really good games.

There was a small store-room at the Anfield Road end of the ground, where we knew we could go and nick a bag of crisps for lunch. Or we'd go over to Eric's little café just facing the ground – it was very cheap and we got to know him well.

We used to enjoy going to Melwood too – Eli Wass is groundsman there and he was a bit more easy-going than Arthur. He would invariably have a big pan of scouse going and you could kick a ball around at break-time.

When the season came round we had to clean the toilets out each week and keep the ground in trim. If the pros had been playing on the Saturday they'd be off on Monday and we'd be out there brushing the stands, cleaning the professionals' boots. They were the old-fashioned tough boots, and we'd have to cut the leather studs for them and tap on the replacements when they were needed.

We had to put the kit out, collect it in, get it dried and brush the boots down. And you didn't go rushing into dressing-rooms – you used to knock on the door and say, 'Excuse me, can I come in?' And you never spoke back to an older pro – you just got on with your work.

I think the process of growing up on the groundstaff has got less involved today. The lads still do certain amount of manual work, but there are other people around to brush the ground, do the painting.

Today's groundstaff lads – well, they call them apprentice professionals today, that's how much the game has changed –

they work very little and do an awful lot of training, which is probably a good thing. But I think they miss out on something. I wouldn't have had it any other way. Eventually I started to enjoy it!

Shankly certainly got things organized at Liverpool. Previously the groundstaff lads didn't do that much training – except maybe with the amateurs up at Melwood on Tuesdays and Thursdays. Lawler and Kinsella, for instance, worked around the ground and would go up to Melwood twice a week to train, then play on Saturdays.

Shankly changed it all round. He employed more groundstaff lads to spread the workload. We would get a rota worked out – five to do the dressing-rooms, hang up the kit, clean out the bath; five to brush the Kop, tidy up the ground. Work that might take you all day you'd finish inside a couple of hours and the rest of the time we trained with the professionals.

Shanks was an awful fellow for neatness and tidiness – if the pitch could have been a perfect green all the year round that would have pleased him. He even used to rope off the piece where you walked on to the ground so you didn't wear out the same strip each week.

Once we were having a practice game at Anfield; we'd had a warm-up round the track and then sat on the wall round the pitch to put our boots on. Quite unconsciously, when I got up I started kicking the ground to make sure they were comfortable and he comes storming over and gives me murder – 'What are you doing? Stop that! You're taking lumps out of the pitch!'

But that was just the sort of fellow he was. He loved every piece of that ground.

I think Shanks had this dream to build a team – perhaps in the back of his mind was the way Matt Busby, whom he admired a lot, had brought up that famous Manchester United side through the junior ranks.

The C team at Anfield then consisted mainly of the groundstaff lads and that year we took the other C teams by storm. Either they felt I was developing quickly or could push on a bit further, but I ended up going from the C team into the B team.

Now the B team was a man's league – we were in the West Cheshire League, playing against Port Sunlight and Cammell Lairds, that sort of thing. It was a bit frightening but maybe they thought I needed stiffening up because that's all it was – just a matter of toughness. Actually, the B team turned out not to be so good as the C team. So I played forward and scored a few goals and the next thing I knew I was in the A team.

The A team consisted of pros who were finishing or younger lads on the way up, mainly over eighteen. The pick of the Tuesday and Thursday amateurs were also included – Chris Lawler, Paddy Kinsella and one or two others I knew.

Anyway I remember we beat Everton 6–1 at Melwood and I scored four, and all of a sudden there was a reserve game at Sheffield United, and I was playing wing-half.

So that year I had about five games as a wing-half or inside-left as a fifteen-year-old and went from the C team to reserves in one season. I enjoyed it – but I found it tiring to go suddenly from thirty-five minutes each way as a schoolboy to playing forty-five minutes each way with the men.

We're talking about the reserves being internationals coming back after injury, playing against pros who are just on the verge of getting into the first team, pros who've just come out of the first team. I enjoyed it – but it's not as though the whole league is made up of fifteen-year-olds.

Chris Lawler had captained Liverpool Schoolboys in 1958–9 and I'd captained them in 1959–60. Chris had also played for English Schoolboys and got every honour you could have wished for. He became my mate because for young lads it was very hard to get involved with the older pros.

Footballers are an unusual breed – they'll be very open with each other and talkative, but the minute an outsider steps in they go quiet. It's very much a closed shop.

They'd been playing together a while anyway and they had their own mates and their own jokes. Callaghan roomed with Gerry Byrne, Ron Yeats, Ian St John, Gordon Milne, Peter Thompson – that sort of thing. They shared things and went out together; something that had happened six months before was still a laugh . . . to try to get in on that was hard for young lads.

Chris was quiet anyway and we found it difficult to get involved. It was about two years before we felt a part of the party.

When I was on the groundstaff we used to go to Melwood for a spot of training. I remember one sunny day we were in the coach going along Liverpool's Queens Drive, where some council workers were digging up the dual carriageway. There was an Evertonian among those lads who used to get a laugh out of us by waving his blue-and-white scarf and shouting after us. He'd be working away there in the sweltering heat with his blue bobblehat on and his Everton scarf, and there was a bit of light-hearted cheering and jeering going on between us.

This happened for a couple of weeks, till one day we went by while he was waiting on the central reservation with a bucket of water, and as we drove past he lobbed the water over the coach.

So the lads got together at Melwood and took a bucket of water along with them on the return journey; as we passed him the bus stopped and one of the lads chucked it all over him. It was really funny; he was standing there in this hole in the road looking like a drowned rat, in his soggy blue-and-white woolly hat.

When I got on the groundstaff I was with Phil Tinney, who lives next door to me now, a lad called Bobby Connolly, who was a little bit older than us, and Gordon Wallace, who now has the garage by the Anfield ground. There was also a lad named Hill whom we used to call Benny. I remember when we went to Newcastle one time to play in a youth game, I roomed with him. He said, 'Can I borrow your toothpaste?' I said, 'Aye, yes, go on.' Well, he picked up my tube of shaving-cream and squeezed it on to his brush. I didn't have the heart to tell him.

Georgie Scott was also with us then – he was terribly unfortunate in the number of appearances he made for the reserves without playing for the first team in the time he spent with Liverpool. At one time we had an important cup game coming up, so the boss picked a number of reserve players for a league match against Wolves, Georgie among them. He managed to get himself injured just a few days before the game!

Bobby Graham played quite a few games for Liverpool, but

he broke his leg and that almost finished his career. Later he moved to Coventry with Ian St John and finished off back in Scotland as an assistant manager.

Phil Tinney went to Dundee eventually and then to America – these were all lads who were on the groundstaff with me. Most of them made it in one way or another.

We had a big goalkeeper called Monty McLaren. Monty was about 6 ft 4 ins and must have weighed 7½ st wringing wet. Benny used to be in digs with him, and he'd come in laughing his head off, telling us how Monty would stand in front of the mirror, admiring himself and making muscles. 'They're just like knots in cotton,' he'd say.

There was an old boy at Anfield called Albert Shelley; he used to play for Liverpool and was the old first-team trainer, but in our day he was just part of the furniture. And he was so funny.

Monty was in the dressing-room one day messing around, and Albert walks in and says, 'Monty, you know what . . . you've got the height, lad, no doubt about that.' And Monty smiles and says, 'Oh yes, I know.' And Albert says, 'And your weight's good too.' And Monty says, 'Oh, thank you very much.' And Albert says, 'And your ability, well that's unquestionable.' Now Monty doesn't know where to put himself. 'All in all,' Albert goes on, 'I'd say you had everything . . . to make the perfect policeman!' And we just fell about. Albert was always taking the mickey and was an expert at sending people up.

There were quite a few Scots on the groundstaff. Whenever we had five-a-side games it was always Scotland *v.* England. We used to get so involved we'd knock lumps out of each other.

The Scotland *v.* England thing used to spill over into our chores and our leisure as well. There was always that extra bit of bravado among the Scots lads. Paddy Kinsella, for instance, used to find it working with Bobby Graham. One day, they were brushing the Kop and Bobby was going on a bit and they almost came to blows. Bobby put his dukes up at Paddy, but he ducked under them easy and Bobby ended up rolling down the Kop steps.

Hamish McKenzie was a cocksure lad as well. I was having a

game of pool one day when Hamish came in with a mate and said he wanted the table. So I just said, 'Wait a minute, we've almost finished.' Well, just for devilment he did the old trick of throwing a few more balls on the table and knackered our game. I went for him, being a hot-tempered lad, and Hamish picked up a cue. 'Okay, come and get me,' he said.

Being a bit crafty as well, I said, 'I'll have a go at you, but put that cue down first.' So he put the cue down . . . and I immediately picked it up myself and belted him with it. But then that was the way with us – you never gave anything or expected anything in return. It was the way we grew up on the groundstaff. It made us tough and it made us fit. There was never any real animosity in the scuffles, and in any case something often happened to defuse the situation pretty quickly. I remember Monty McLaren, all 6 ft 4 ins of him and built like a beanpole, put his dukes up to me once so I butted him on the nose and he went down. I went down too, on top of him, and the next thing is he's shouting, 'Let me up, you daft sod – you're spoiling my new suit.' And we both started laughing.

The older pros, in fact, rarely spoke to you. You trained with the pros, but you didn't look up to anyone, mainly because in 1960 there was nobody to look up to.

Of course there was always Billy Liddell. I idolized Billy, but he was coming to the end of his career then. I actually played one or two games with him in the reserves. Billy was thirty-six then, and he was the idol when we were at school – it was Billy at Anfield and Peter Farrall at Everton. It was a real disappointment to join Liverpool and find Billy didn't get carried around like the Pope.

But what people don't realize is that you can get so intent on your own training you haven't time to chat to those around you. You can get an older pro who won't say a word to you for years. Some might say 'you're doing that wrong' and give you the odd spot of advice, but basically they train to their own system and it's the trainers who are there to coach you. I joined the groundstaff in May but I didn't touch a ball for six weeks. The first pro I saw was Ian St John. I didn't recognize him from Adam and thought he'd come to fix the electrics or something.

When I first joined, Shanks had just had a clearout; Tommy Younger and Barry Wilkinson had left, and the team consisted of Bert Slater in goal, Dick White, Gerry Byrne, Johnny Molyneux, Johnny Wheeler . . . then they bought big Ron Yeats same time as I joined, and Ian St John. Cally had just started playing, and there was a lad named Bobby Campbell, who became manager of Fulham. Billy Liddell was still there, Dave Hickson, Alan A'Court, Jimmy Melia, Johnny Morrisey, Roger Hunt . . . then they bought Gordon Milne, and Willie Stevenson . . . Ronnie Moran was still in the team when I joined, then Shanks bought a lad named Kevin Lewis and sold him again, bought a goalkeeper, Jimmy Furnell, and Peter Thompson.

Liverpool were a Second Division team then, but in Shanks's first full season they won the League and gained promotion. The following year they were in the semi-finals of the FA Cup, the year after that they won the League, and the next year the FA Cup. That was the season I started playing full-time for the first team – 1964–5.

Everton, of course, were already in the First Division – they had gone up the year Liverpool went down – 1954 – so it was the first year we'd been in the same division for ten years or so.

I never considered joining Everton from school. Everton never interested me. I think if your dad is a Liverpudlian, you are a Liverpudlian. It's very rare you get a switch.

I used to nip off from school to see the last quarter of the game at Anfield – they used to play in the afternoons then because they had no floodlights and at three-quarter time you could get in free. I remember standing at the back of the Kop and watching Billy Liddell score against Manchester City in the Cup. But the referee disallowed it, because he said he'd already blown for time.

Anfield has changed completely since I knew it as a kid. From being a Second Division club and ground it's now one of the best in Europe – no question about that. The dressing-room facilities are good, the pitch is good, the ground holds fifty-odd thousand.

When I went to Goodison first it was to watch a schools final and I went right up into the stands. People say going to Goodison is like watching the game on television – all you get is a good aerial view. I found out the stands at Everton were so high you could get nosebleed if you got to the top!

The fans always seem a long way from you at Goodison – at Anfield they're on top of you. Anfield was always a more homely ground, a ground for atmosphere.

Everton's School of Science reputation is a lot of bull, but what they did at Everton was clap every time someone did something good. At Liverpool they'd shout and cheer – that was the main difference. Goodison was for gentlemen, so they said!

4 The Men and the Boys

If it had been at all possible I would like to have seen a match between the Liverpool team of the mid-1960s and the 1970s side. They were two very different teams with very different styles, but both were extremely effective in their day.

Talking about the likes of Gerry Byrne, the only person I've ever seen give Gerry a roasting was little Willie Henderson who played for Scotland when Gerry played for England. But usually Gerry could take care of himself.

Chris Lawler was without doubt the best goal-scoring full-back you could ever wish to see, while in goal Tommy Lawrence for two or three seasons was the best keeper in the world. Sadly, something happened to him and he went down. He was one of the nicest fellows I've ever met.

For five years big Ron Yeats was the best centre-half in the world, easy, and Willie Stevenson the best clipper of a ball I've ever seen. He wasn't a defender, more a lazy midfield player, and really the best clipper around.

Gordon Milne, for his work-rate and for everything he did, finally got his dues when he played for England. Then when Liverpool won the FA Cup in 1965 Geoff Strong, who came from Arsenal, played for Milne in the final, when Gordon was injured. Geoff was the original utility player, he could stand in for anyone, and he was more than useful to the Liverpool team in those days.

Then there was Ian St John; if you were selling him now you could ask more than £1 million, no problem. He was one of the greatest players I've ever known. Same with Roger Hunt – I've never known anyone score goals or get into positions like him.

They used to compare Roger with Jimmy Greaves – now Jimmy was a great goal-scorer, but Roger was a goal-scorer and a great worker as well.

Then there was Tony Hateley . . . Shanks also made his mistakes. He thought the sun shone out of Tony Hateley's behind, yet within eighteen months Tony had been and gone. Shanks found out he wasn't as good a player as he thought. Hateley was a great header of a ball but he didn't fit in with the rest of Shankly's plans.

Shanks also sold Willy Carlin to Derby County. He was a good little player. I well remember him on the day County thrashed us 4–0 at Derby and I can still see the smile on Willy's face now. He was a great little fellow.

If you're talking about real talent, you can't omit Peter Thompson – we used to give him the ball and let him play with it for five minutes while we had a rest. For ball-control he was magic.

Probably one of the best players who ever played for Liverpool is Cally. In all the years he was at Anfield, Ian Callaghan had only one poor season, when he had his cartilage out. I remember giving him stick one day at Crystal Palace – I'll regret that till the day I die. I had a go at him and there's no way you can have a go at Cally – he always tries, but this particular day his leg must have been giving him hell and I didn't realize it.

If you're talking about the 1970s team, you're talking about Clem. There were only two goalkeepers at Liverpool while I was there – Tommy Lawrence and Ray Clemence. Clem is the best in the world, no doubt about that. He trains hard, but he has the advantage of natural ability. At times it is unbelievable.

Liverpool sold Alec Lindsay but he still had the best left foot

I've ever seen; it was tremendous. They used to say he could open cans with it.

If Larry Lloyd could have controlled himself he would probably still be at Liverpool too, but he always seemed to lack something. Larry got left out of the side, and in practice games at Melwood started kicking his own team-mates. Mind you, he picked his players. I remember Ray Kennedy joining the club and playing in a practice game – reserves *v.* the first team – when Larry gave him a right wellying, first minute. Shanks had to halt the game and pull him off. Larry was sold soon after that.

We used to call Larry 'Albert Tatlock', because he'd be moaning all the time. When he first came to Liverpool I, being captain, took him to my house for a meal – he was a nice fellow but he was an awful moaner. The sort of fellow who'd get up in the morning and if it was sunny would say, 'Argh! It's not raining,' and if it was raining, 'Argh! It's not sunny.' Whatever it was he would want the opposite. We'd be out for a meal and you'd stick fish and chips in front of him and he'd say, 'I want steak.' Give him steak and he'd say he wanted something else. You couldn't win.

Kevin Keegan said in his book that I had a go at him at Melwood – that wasn't true. I may have called him a little twerp once in a while if he climbed all over me during a five-a-side or something, but we never came to blows.

It was me and Larry Lloyd who almost came to blows – he used to think he could get away with murder. He'd been playing up once and at the last minute I stopped myself from butting him, but only just. I reckon my head ended up about six inches from his nose.

I know my reputation as a player who wouldn't stand any nonsense came about from incidents on the park – some were true, some exaggerated and some attributed to me, though someone else was to blame.

I remember one time at Melwood in training when we were having a five-a-side and I was on the same side as Ian St John. We scored a goal and Tony Hateley went to fetch the ball from behind the posts. In his frustration he gave the ball a mighty kick and wellied it, accidentally, into the back of Ian's head. St John was round in a flash and grabbed hold of Tony, and everyone could see there was going to be a fight. I was the nearest person to them so I stepped in between them to try and stop it. Tony now thinks that I'm picking on him as well, so he turns to me and says, 'Keep out of it, or I'll have you and all . . .' and puts his fists up.

Straight away, no messing, before he could start anything I whacked him in the face and he went down – then it was Ian picking me off Tony. Word of that soon got round. Tony was as good as gold really, but these things happen in the heat of the moment.

Ray Kennedy came to Liverpool disillusioned with Arsenal, though I never really knew why. At Arsenal he used to look up to Frank McLintock a lot and when Frank left he seemed none too happy. Some players need other players to look up to, to give them that extra will to win. McLintock was Arsenal to a certain extent and when he left the team seemed to fall apart.

Ray had done quite well at Arsenal and won a UEFA Cup medal as well as helping them do the double, but when he came to Anfield he was overweight and I think he'd lost interest in the game. When he had sorted out who he could trust, he used to confide in Cally and I and take his cue from us. Once he'd settled in and Liverpool had switched his position he became one of the best midfielders we've ever had. He's a truly tremendous player.

John Toshack and Kevin Keegan as a duo were magic. In fact they complemented each other so well they had tests run on the both of them to see if they were telepathic. But it was just that Tosh was a big lad, good in the air, and Kevin was so quick off the mark he could pick up the ball anywhere. Tosh's game was natural; it was a joy to watch, and he made Kevin look good. Kevin, in fact, struggled a little bit in the England side because there was no one to do for him what Tosh could do effortlessly. He was expected to do it all himself.

But Kevin's always had his head screwed on right. If you're talking about players worth £1 million, Kevin's like the Mona

Lisa – beyond price. I admire Kevin for making full use of what he had. He could so easily have been another Georgie Best, who squandered and wasted his talents. Kevin was a much more stable lad, but he annoyed several people when he left by not levelling with them. All that about broadening his experience in Europe was just so much smoke-screen – he went for the money pure and simple. And if he'd come out and said it no one would have thought any the less of him, but he acted as though he was ashamed of it.

Terry McDermott, to my mind, was just happy to be around at Anfield for the first twelve months. He was a Liverpool lad who'd gone to Bury and on to Newcastle, then he'd come back to Liverpool and he was just happy for that fact, overjoyed at being asked to join a team which had whacked Newcastle in the Cup the year before. He's a good player, though, is Terry – does a lot of running but gets disheartened very quickly.

Liverpool bought Kenny Dalglish to replace Keegan. Kenny's got the best feint I've seen in a long time – he's brilliant at sending people the wrong way. In fact he sometimes looks awkward, but he's not. Everything he does is planned and he does it with determination.

Then they bought Grahame Souness. When we used to play Middlesbrough the boss would say, 'Well, they've only got Souness playing anyway. He's all you've got to worry about.' Then Liverpool went out and bought him so Middlesbrough had nothing! He's a good distributor of the ball, probably lacks a little bit of ability in defensive situations, but one of his main assets is going forward.

Jimmy Case is an important part of Liverpool's set-up now. He's one of the better players and it's a pity he hasn't got what he deserves in the way of England honours. Jimmy attacks, defends, does the lot – he's like a young Cally really.

I rate Davey Fairclough a twenty-minute player because he'll do as much in twenty minutes as he's going to do in ninety, so you've got an unfortunate situation where, if you can put up with seventy minutes of frustration, Davey's going to do something special in the remaining twenty.

It's a bit psychological with Davey – he's done things in ten minutes of coming on in his supersub days that were pure magic, but I've played a full game with him and he hasn't done a tap. I say he's got one Stan Stennett leg and one Charlie Chaplin leg, because he falls over the ball that many times before putting it in the back of the net! But Davey's all right, and basically a good player.

Alan Hansen developed into a good player but took his time to settle down. He needed brainwashing, if you like, to make him appreciate just how good a player he was. He never seemed to get totally involved, or be fully aware of what was going on around him, but now his confidence has grown and he gets much more excited about things.

Steve Heighway, coming to us as a college lad and straight from playing amateur football, had quite a bit to learn regarding attitudes. I know for a fact that it's embarrassing for him to recall those days now – soon after he joined us he did an article for a magazine in which he said, 'Football isn't all my life. I could give it up tomorrow . . .' and we used to take the mick out of him for this something cruel. He was so idealistic it was untrue. Now he gets as upset as anybody if Liverpool lose and enjoys his games – more than that he cares how we play. One time he would put pressure on you in a way, because he didn't give a damn if Liverpool won or lost.

I remember coming back from Crystal Palace with Steve on the train. He hadn't been with us long, and he was sitting with Jack Whitham; we were playing cards and vaguely listening to them talking and I think Steve was genuinely looking for a bit of sympathy. To hear the two of them talk you'd have thought they'd been sitting in the stands all afternoon, not involved in the game on the pitch.

I got quite excited and told them what I thought of them – my anger was more directed at Steve's ignorance. I'd tell them, 'If I had to rely on you for my bonus I'd be skint by the end of the year. But if you're relying on me, you'll make a couple of bob. . . .'

Like I say, Steve is a totally different player now, fully committed, but it was a lesson he had to learn the hard way, because, quite frankly when he joined Liverpool he was a bit of a bore. It wasn't just that he was a college lad – Brian Hall came from college, too, yet from the word go he could get stuck in, and get depressed or annoyed if we lost.

It was nice to get college lads in the side – it proved to people that not all footballers are absolute idiots, though I know there were those who used to treat us like idiots anyway.

Jack Whitham was quite incredible – he was a total hypochondriac, the sort of person you wouldn't take with you to visit anyone in hospital, because he would probably end up in the next bed. . . . If there was a flu epidemic in China he'd catch it before anyone else. He used to pull a muscle one day, then be running like hell the next. It got to a point where even the trainers would look at him a bit funny.

He was so naive, too. He moved out to Formby when he was with us, and we used to pull his leg. 'Not much to do out there, Jack, no picture houses, only a couple of decent pubs, nowhere to go socially . . . mind you, we hear there's quite a few good key parties around. . . .'

And he didn't know what the hell we were talking about, so we said, 'You know, Jack. Don't you ever get invited along to throw your keys in?' He said, 'Listen, if you think I'm going to let any stranger drive my new car around you've got another think coming.' And all the lads groaned.

Every club has one, I guess, and maybe every club needs one, for people like Jack take the tension off, ease your own mind off being injured, help you relax.

Over the years the atmosphere at Anfield became more relaxed as we became more successful. At one time there was nowhere you could go and sit, no proper players' lounge, and if you went into the dining-room perhaps the roof would be leaking. But Shanks was responsible for a lot of the changes that made Anfield more relaxing, and more accessible to the fans.

The Kop tradition has always been at Anfield. As a kid I would go and stand in the Kop – it always had that special aura about it. And it got noticed in the 1960s when Liverpool started winning things, the same as the Stretford End at Manchester United when they started winning things. That's why people probably don't say the same things about Everton, because there's nothing special connected with Goodison. And they haven't won so many things in the past few years – it's as simple as that.

If you were to say to me, 'I'll meet you outside the Goodison Road entrance at five,' I'd probably have to walk all round the ground to make sure I had the right place. Even going there and playing there – and in my early days I scored a hat-trick at Goodison playing for Lancashire Schoolboys – I know it's a decent ground, but it's never held anything for me.

I've had some terrific laughs at Anfield. Once a fellow threw a pork chop, raw, on to the pitch for me, shortly after the game started. Must have thought it was feeding-time for 'Animal' Smith!

When I first started playing, as a youngster among men, I soon realized the way to win was to frighten the opposition. So I used to growl at them, and show my teeth – what's left of them – and it seemed to work. It was a tough-guy reputation that took me about twelve months to forge, and twelve years to live down. I don't think I've ever lived it down.

Anyway I used to get stick from the stands for this. And at Anfield the Kemlyn Road stand is so close you can almost go up and pick them out. This particular day there's one lad giving me chat and chancing his arm, so I went over and barked, 'Okay, which one of you is it?' And they're all pointing in different directions – 'It's him. Not me. It's him!' So I said something like, 'I'll get you after. Just you wait.' But in fact I never bothered.

Sometimes you can mis-kick a ball and it goes out of play, and you go across to pick it up and they'll say, 'Oh Christ, can't you kick it better than that? What sort of a ball was that?' So you say to them, 'Take your coat off and give it to me. Then I'll get in the stand and you come down here and have a game. See if you can do any better. . . .'

I never used to do it when I first started. I'd just growl at the crowd, or tell them to 'sod off'. But later I got to like chatting with the crowd – and with other players.

I remember one year we played against Coventry on a Saturday morning – it was Grand National Day so we played in the morning – and they had Tommy Hutchinson playing for them, who also played for Scotland. Well, that day he was absolutely pathetic.

We got a penalty in the first half and Alec Lindsay scored from it at the Anfield Road end. We were running back to the centre when Tommy passes me and says, 'That's the worst penalty I've seen in my life!' So I said, 'It hit the back of the net. What more do you want?' Tommy thinks I'm getting cheeky, thinks I'm having a go at him, so he says, 'Tell you what, I'll race you back to the centre for your wages.' Well, I've never been able to run quickly in my life, but I can take care of myself, so I suggested, 'Only if we double it up after the race, and have a scrap so I can knock the hell out of you.' He didn't want to know then.

But I liked taking the mick out of him. It was all good fun. Scotland were going to the World Cup that year in West Germany, so one time the ball went out of play by the Paddock, and I was chatting to the crowd . . . 'Are there any Scotsmen among you? See that fellow over there. He's going to Germany next month, he's going to play in the World Cup, and he can't even get past me!' The crowd loved it but Tommy was getting madder and madder. There's nothing worse than getting het-up when you're playing football, because nothing goes right for you after that.

But Tommy's really a good lad – it's just that things tended to happen like that when I was playing.

Our own lads and the staff used to take the mick as well, not least old Albert Shelley. I remember once when he was in the dug-out during a reserves Derby game with Everton at Goodison and we were 3–0 down in a quarter of an hour. The ball went out of play and rolled into the dug-out, so I went over for the ball to take the throw-in and there's Albert saying, 'Smithy, sit down here, son. This is the worst game I've ever seen anyone play. Leave the ball, forget it, tell them to call the game off . . .' He went muttering on like that and in the end I had to reach into the dug-out and fetch the ball myself. There was no way Albert was going to do it for me.

Then there was Bobby Campbell – he used to do terrific imitations of Shanks. We used to take the kit down of an afternoon and give it out at Melwood for pre-session training. It was bundled into a couple of sacks in those days and you used to dip in for whatever you needed. There wasn't a proper drying-room at Anfield then, so the kit at the bottom of the bag was probably never thoroughly dried anyway. One day I was giving the boots out and ended up with the last kit in the bag, and it was soaking. So I said, 'Excuse me, this kit's soaking wet, like.' So Bobby, in his best Shanks voice, says, 'Eeh, hang on laddie, you have mine . . .' So he gives me his, and it's worse than the one I picked. That taught me a lesson.

Superstitions have always been a part of the game. I used to have quite a lot, till the day I got dropped by Shanks. Then I dropped the lot of them and didn't give a hell what happened!

It was all psychological. I'd put my boots on in a certain way, fasten them in a certain way, throw a hairbrush to Chris Lawler, taking a programme with me if I went to the toilet. Even from getting up in the morning I had to do a certain crossword, do this, do that . . . it was unbelievable and looking back it just all seems pretty silly. Even the players' wives used to get involved. My wife Susie, the year we went to Rome, got into the habit of eating spaghetti with the children before our European Cup games. They must have put on pounds eating the stuff – and I suppose you could say it worked.

Attitudes change a lot over the years too. I know when Liverpool first got to Wembley, the wives would dread the semi-finals in case we got beat. 'We don't care what happens at Wembley, so long as we get there,' they used to say. Looking back, it seemed a stupid thing to say – of course they wanted us to win – especially at Wembley. But then over the years we got to Wembley so many times that Sue told me she became sick of the place. I know that sounds dreadful, but she began to hate the tension of the big occasion – and then again she saw me being beaten more times than she saw me win at Wembley.

But you have to experience defeat at that level to appreciate victory, and the one occasion that made up for everything else was that magic night in Rome. Sue must have smoked the best part of two packs of cigarettes during that final, and when I scored, was so elated and tearful, she could have sat in that stadium till the dawn broke.

5 First Taste of Success

I never really had a settled position in my early days at Anfield. At school I used to play centre-half or centre-forward and I joined Liverpool as a centre-forward in the C team. I was still a forward in the B team and I was getting goals – we beat General Chemicals one time about 6–2 and I scored four, and when we were beaten by Hoylake 5–4 I scored three.

By the time I got to the reserves I was playing right-half – that was against Sheffield United when I was fifteen. I played about five reserve games that year, then the following year I was in the reserves from the word go – at left-half or inside-left.

I remember feeling grieved sometimes at not being part of the C team, which was Shanks's 'baby' – he seemed to be grooming them, mainly groundstaff lads, into his team of the future, and even though I'd progressed to reserve-team football I always had a sneaking feeling I should be part of his 'favourite' squad. Mind you, he used me to tell the C team lads what it was like to play on league grounds – because by then I'd played at Villa and Sheffield United . . . real big-time stuff.

They used to have pre-season Reds *v.* Whites games at Anfield – the first team were the Reds and the reserves were Whites. I was sixteen and came on in the second half and scored a goal, heading it straight in from a corner. They had an inquest about that goal on the Monday, asking me how I'd scored it, because I had to climb above big Ronnie Yeats to nod it in! I just said I'd nipped in and caught it right – I didn't have any secret plan to divulge, it was just one of those things. Anyway it certainly impressed Shanks. Mind you, the reserves still lost 2–1, Roger Hunt scoring both times for the Reds.

At the age of seventeen I was switched to wing-half and used to mark Jimmy Melia, who was always inside-left. Jimmy wasn't the bravest lad in the world, and me being robust and not taking nonsense from anybody, meant I was more or less free to play as I wished. The other lads used to say it was Jimmy as much as anybody who helped me get into the first team, because he didn't really want to know.

I was seventeen when I made my début with the first team. What happened was we were playing Birmingham at the end of the season and they were near the bottom of the League with Manchester United. It had been announced that we were resting one or two internationals and playing several youngsters – myself, Gordon Wallace and Bobby Graham. So Manchester United lodged a protest that we were fielding a weakened side, because it was vital Liverpool won the Birmingham game. If Birmingham got two points, Manchester United could maybe have gone down instead.

They needn't really have bothered – we battered Birmingham 5–1, and United didn't even send us a congratulation wire!

But once I'd played in the first team I thought that's it – I'm in. Especially as I'd already been disappointed the previous month, when Jimmy Melia was injured and wasn't fit for our FA Cup semi-final with Leicester at Hillsborough. There was talk in the papers that I might play, and I was sat there in the dressing-room wanting to go to the toilet every five minutes, I was that keyed up. Then Shanks came in and said he was playing Chris Lawler instead – funny thing was I suddenly felt okay, and it was Chris who was up and down to the toilet!

Anyway, we then came up to a mid-week game against Sheffield Wednesday at home, and Shanks said to me at lunchtime, 'Go home and get ready. You're playing.'

When I got back to the ground Jimmy Melia was there, talking to Johnny Wheeler who'd been out looking at the pitch, and he asked Jimmy how he felt. Jimmy was always a cocky lad and was saying, 'I don't know if I'll play a full game . . . mind you, sixty minutes of me is better than ninety minutes of anybody else.' In the end, contrary to what Shanks had told me, Jimmy did play – and we got beat 2–0, so he might as well have not bothered.

I felt so disillusioned, especially with Shanks. He wasn't one for giving explanations for his actions, and I was so eager to get into the first team, I just felt angry and confused. What I should have realized was that Jimmy was on his way out and all I needed was patience – but then I've never been a patient sort of fellow.

Rumours were also reaching Chris Lawler and myself that Manchester United, who were still rebuilding their side after the 1958 Munich tragedy, had offered £50,000 for the pair of us. But we never heard anything officially and nothing ever came of it.

I didn't get a regular first-team place the following season either, but I was learning all the time. The game was made up of real characters then, men you felt you could talk to for days, and not just about football, men I grew to respect.

I also got a few rude awakenings. News of my hard way of playing got around, and I remember playing Chesterfield reserves one time when I was in the England Youth side, and one of their tough defenders singled me out for a slanging match . . . 'England Youth ! You couldn't pop a hole in a paper bag !' We beat them 5–0 for all that.

We played Chesterfield at Anfield, and that was also the first time I got into trouble. I was having a go at the linesman, and he couldn't find the ball . . . only because I'd stuck it up my shirt. I'm afraid the ref didn't think that very funny and I was booked.

Other things helped to spread my reputation. One fellow, Frank Clark, playing for Newcastle reserves then, broke his ankle playing against me – not through dirty play, it was just one of those things. We went into a tackle together and I just heard a slap, like someone smacking your leg, and that was it. I've spoken to Frank many times since and he accepts it was a pure accident. It didn't really do him any harm, because he ended up playing for Nottingham Forest and winning a European Cup winners' medal with them in 1979.

One of the things that used to be said about me was 'Tommy breaks your back . . .' Well, Frankie was the only player I tangled with who ever broke anything during my career.

The FA Cup is the one trophy most teams want to win – it's the one with all the charisma attached to it. Next to the First Division Championship the Cup is the focal point of the season.

In recent years they've tried to build up the League Cup, but it's just a sort of consolation prize – it hasn't the tradition or the glamour attached to it that the FA Cup has. Maybe it would be better if they played it on a special day instead of an ordinary League day, and promoted it more. Clubs in the lower divisions seem to have a better chance of doing well in the League Cup competition and there's the added bonus these days of playing in the final at Wembley, as well as entry into Europe, so all the time it's gaining in momentum.

But you ask most clubs – League and non-League – which competition they would want to do best in and they'll tell you the FA Cup. It's got surprises, giant-killers, suspense – the lot.

The 1965 Cup final came at the end of the first season in which I played continuous first-team football for Liverpool and of course it was also the first time Liverpool FC won the Cup, which made it doubly memorable for me.

You always get the feeling that you're going to win, that it's your lucky streak, and I remember going to play Spurs at White Hart Lane about a week before the final; for relaxation we'd gone to the White City Stadium to watch the dogs and I'd lost a few quid that night and had to borrow a fiver for the last race. I didn't honestly know one end of a dog from the other, but I thought I'd go mad for the last race and bet the fiver with the one I had left on a three-dog twist forecast, picking nos 1, 3 and 5 at random.

Now no. 5 was a pure outsider who happened to lead all the way round and romped home and there was a photo for second between no. 3 who was the favourite and another outsider, no. 1. They gave it to no. 1, and when the odds were worked out I ended up with something like £137 for my stake, which was a small fortune to me in those days.

But it all added up to this feeling that we couldn't lose, that it had to be our year. I had a good final as it happened, even though I don't remember everything about it, but two or three things stand out in my mind. We played Leeds and they had a coloured winger called Albert Johannson. The ball was coming down their left wing, and he and I both went for it – but he did a detour, chickened out of meeting me. Don Revie had great faith in Johannson, though, and kept shouting to his midfield, 'Find the black man. Find the black!' Bob Paisley got a bit fed up with this after a while so he told him 'They can't – he's snookered behind our white!' Which was true.

I also remember discussing with Willie Stevenson afterwards over who nodded the ball down for the Bremner goal. He thought it was me, but when I saw the television replay later, I knew I was right. It wasn't.

I also remember Gerry Byrne did his collar-bone in the opening minutes of the game and played virtually the whole final with it broken. I don't know if he realized it or not, but he played as though there were nothing wrong with him at all.

And, of course, I remember Cally – I can still see him steaming down the wing. Peter Thompson had got involved in the game and had pushed the ball through to me. I had given it to Cally, who did all the running, crossed it and Ian St John put it in the net.

Like I said, we felt it had to be our season. We'd had a good Cup run – we'd beaten Stockport County, then we'd drawn Leicester, who were always a bogey side, and we'd beaten them in the replay; we hammered Chelsea in the semis, and now at Wembley the idol of the Kop had scored, and so had Roger Hunt, another of their idols; he'd also capped that season by playing for England.

We all felt it was the start of something special, more so than when we won the League the year before. But then, of course, our European semi-final encounters with Inter-Milan were still to come, so the season didn't end on quite the high note it should have done.

But at least we'd won the Cup, and we got a tremendous

reception when we came back to Liverpool Town Hall. There were people hanging from windows, lamp-posts, everywhere – it was just fantastic, unreal, and a bit frightening. But it was a scene we were to become familiar with during the 1960s and 1970s.

I don't suppose it dawned on me what we'd done till afterwards. Then it felt magic to know that Liverpool had won the Cup for the first time and I'd been part of it. After all, I was only a lad of twenty.

In football there's usually something to bring you down to earth. I remember once being really made up because I put a couple of penalties past Pat Jennings when I played for England Youth against the rest of Great Britain at Wembley. We were playing before thirty to forty thousand people, I scored one in each half and we hammered them 5–2. The following weekend I was playing at Huddersfield for Liverpool reserves against Huddersfield reserves in front of thirty or forty people, and I had to take a penalty again – and I missed it. Joe Fagan pulled my leg about that for years.

When I got picked for regional trials for the England Youth team I had to go to Manchester. Colin Harvey was among the trialists, and he gave me a lift home. After that I got picked for the full England Youth trials at Leamington Spa.

That was the first time I met Alan Ball. We ended up in the Possibles *v.* Probables game together. I was right-half, and he came round before the game telling me I ought to get stuck into their inside-left, so he could nip through easier. Well, it was only trials, and I began to wonder why the hell he needed my help to prove he was a good player. I had my own way to make – I wasn't going to kick the hell out of the opposition for him. I know he's turned into a good player since then, but the fact was that I got picked for the England Youth side and Bally got the bullet.

Our manager was a lad named Pat Welton, who is now on Tottenham's staff, and Wilf McGuinness was the England Youth trainer. We used to get together maybe once a month and have practice games against Sheffield United Under-20s, Notts

Forest Under-23s, that sort of thing, and in the end we built up quite a squad.

I remember one game at Coventry, when we were beaten 2–1 after leading 1–0 till something like the 85th minute; when we came back Pat Welton had an inquest. It was the first time I'd come across Londoners making excuses . . . I've come across it a lot since then, but this was the first.

We had Ray Bloomfield in our side then – his brother used to play for the Arsenal. He'd been playing inside-right and I was right-half. During the game the Coventry midfielder had been giving him a hell of a time. Coventry had an older, more experienced side and they were using an inside-forward who was deep-lying. He was going so far back into their area to pick up balls that to pick him up I would have had to spend three quarters of the game in their half and be right out of my position for much of the time. We were also trying out a 4–4–2 system and there was really no way I was going to get drawn out of my rôle in that line-up.

So at the inquest afterwards, when all the excuses started coming out and Ray started blaming me for not picking up this fellow, I told him straight, 'You should have picked him up. You could see what was happening. He was as much your responsibility as mine.' I wasn't necessarily just getting at Ray – it was a case of tactics. Whether my reading of the situation went down well or not I don't know, but I ended up in Pat Welton's squad again, and Ray didn't.

We went to Switzerland, too, and played a Swiss Under-21 side, beating them 2–0 comfortably. It was during this game that I got knocked out by Ronnie Harris of Chelsea. We'd both gone up for a header and he butted me, so I had to come off. That night the others went off to watch an ice-hockey game, and Wilf sat with me with an ice-pack on my head. I get migraine these days – one of the many legacies of a football career – and I'm sure it started after that collision with Ronnie.

We finished off that year – 1963 – entering the International Youth tournament. It was the first time England had entered with a team of first-year pros. In previous years we'd always fielded amateurs. Nowadays it's called the Junior World Cup, but in those days it just meant that players who'd been a couple of years with League sides, playing in the reserves or being the local wonderboy or whatever, had that little bit of experience that counted.

In our side we had Johnny Cowan, who was a goalkeeper with Chelsea. He was brilliant and why he never made it I'll never know. I think he tossed a coin in the end, and ended up a golfer.

Right-back was Lennie Badger, who played for Sheffield United and later for England and was a hell of a player. Only a slight lad, but a classic full-back; he had an unfortunate break of the leg after he left Sheffield but he picked up several international caps.

Left-back was Bernie Shaw, who also played for Sheffield United and later moved to Wolves – a good lad. Centre-half was Lou Chatterley, a big lad from Villa, and left-half was Ronnie Harris, who was our captain. Maybe he and I gave the team the professional look that year, because we were both hard-tackling wing-halves with similar reputations.

In the forward line at outside-right was Graham French; inside-right was Johnny Sammels, who played for Arsenal; centre-forward was George Jones, who played for Bury, and later on for Blackburn and Southport; inside-left was John Sissons, of West Ham; and outside-left was Ray Whittaker, also of Arsenal. And we had David Sadler and David Pleat among the subs – a great bunch of players.

In our group we played our first game against the Netherlands at Wimbledon and beat them 6–0, no problem. Second game we played the trophy-holders, Romania, who hadn't been beaten for two years. We played them at Highbury and just tore them apart, winning 3–0. The third game in our group was with Russia, and as we had such a good goal aggregate Pat rested several players, me included, but we still beat them 2–0. Phil Beale, of Spurs, was our reserve defender and he took my place.

So the semi-finals were between the winners of the four groups – that was us, with Northern Ireland, Scotland and Bulgaria. We played Scotland at White City Stadium and beat them 1–0, getting to the final without conceding a goal. Scotland also had a decent side that year – Peter Lorimer was in it, I remember. Northern Ireland drew their game with Bulgaria, and they reached Wembley on the toss of a coin – what a way to win!

At Wembley we couldn't put a foot wrong. We got four goals past Pat Jennings that afternoon and still didn't let one in. That England Youth side was the first I played with that tasted a bit of real glory, and that Junior World Cup trophy was the first honour I won playing with fellows from other clubs.

We'd been staying at Bognor Regis at a holiday camp during the tournament, alongside players from the other competing countries; I think it was the Italians who were nearest to us and, when they got back from having a few drinks one night, there was a bit of a rumpus. It ended up with them throwing water over each other for a laugh, but it threatened to turn a bit nasty, and disrupted the whole block.

So Wilf McGuinness, our trainer, came in and said, 'I'm going to sort this little lot out. Who's coming with me?' He meant he was off to protest to their team manager and get them quietened down, but I thought he meant he was off to start fighting them, so I said, 'All right then,' and I whipped my shirt off and was half-way down the hall all ready to knock hell out of them. Wilf couldn't tell for laughing whether I was serious or not. However it all got sorted out peacefully, and Wilf and I still have a laugh about it when I see him.

Because we won this trophy they took us away to the Canary Isles for a week – and that was my first brush with foreigners. We played a Las Palmas XI and beat them 3–2, then we played a Canary Islands representative team and were coasting 1–0 when they decided to send somebody off, and they picked on poor Ray Whittaker. In the end they beat us 2–1, with a couple of dubious goals, but I suppose they thought honour had been satisfied.

It was while we were relaxing on the island one night that we goaded George Jones into drinking a bottle of Scotch. He said, 'I'm not doing it for nothing' so we each threw a nicker in – there were about eight of us – and he began to drink the whole bottle.

I've never seen anybody get so drunk so fast in my life. It was a mad thing to do – he could have killed himself, but none of us realized that, because none of us were hard drinkers. I think he got about a third of the way down and that was it – we had to put him to bed.

They got the team back together again the following season to play a UK side. Pat Jennings was in goal again for the opposition, and we beat them 5–2. I scored twice from the penalty spot. That team was the first one I played for that actually won anything worth having. We were brilliant!

6 Give the Lad a Break

I learnt an important lesson about injuries early on in my playing career. We were playing Newcastle and it was a typically hard game, when their big centre-forward Wyn Davies powered through our defence and knocked the goalkeeper, Tommy Lawrence, for six.

He was lying there in the penalty area, with a gash on his knee, and it was getting near half-time, so the trainer, Bob Paisley, knew there was no way he was going to get taken off. He kidded Tommy along that it was only a scratch, and the other players reassured him too.

Then I bounded over and without thinking, took one look at the cut and said: 'Urrgh! That's terrible! Needs at least three stitches!' Well, Tommy turned white and Bob rounded on me and slung a dripping wet sponge in my face.

The crowd thought it was a huge joke – but it taught me that when it comes to injuries, yours or anybody else's, keep your mouth shut and never let it show.

I was only fifteen when I first discovered the agony of being really injured, and what a boring, frustrating time it can be for any player. It was also my first contact with hard men in the game, harder than I've ever been. . . .

I remember a game against Aston Villa reserves. Nigel Sims was in goal and they had a brawny full-back called Stan Lynn, who came up to me and threatened to knock my head off. He said he'd knock hell out of me if I came anywhere near him. I thought, 'That's not nice . . .'

Anyway there was a ball going spare across the box and I dived on it to try and put it in the back of the net, and they were both coming at me, Sims and Lynn. In fact Nigel came off his line with his feet and nearly knocked my kneecap off. It was bloody painful.

What they used to do in those days if you had a knock on the knee was smother it in thick Vaseline, wrap an old towel round it, bathe it in really hot water till you could bear it no more, then throw cold water over it.

This hot-and-cold treatment was supposed to reduce the swelling, which it did, but what it did mostly was get your trousers all greasy, because you could never get rid of all that Vaseline in one wash – it would cling to everything.

In fact, over the years, you learn to treat your own injuries with these simple remedies. I also remember when I didn't play in the European Cup final at Wembley against Bruges because I'd broken a toe; I ended up on the kitchen draining-board throwing hot-and-cold over it. But I soon learnt that though it might work for a bruising it's the worst thing you can do for a break. My foot went from a size 9 to a size 14 in no time!

With the number of games Liverpool played in a year I reckon I was pretty lucky with injuries. I didn't have that many breaks. I broke a kneecap and I broke that toe (though that had nothing to do with football) and I fractured a few bits of finger and ribs, but basically that's it apart from pulled muscles, and you usually get over those pretty quickly.

All the same if you average that out against the number of games you play in a season you find you don't have that much time to relax and get over injuries properly. Even in later years when I wasn't playing all the season for Liverpool, I still played in the States in the summer and averaged the same number of games in a year.

Obviously, you tend to play with injuries – they are just a hazard of the game. I've played with stitches in my mouth, my head, even in my legs, though a lot of people think I just dish it out. But the drawback about being the hard man of the side is you're not supposed to show it when you get injured, and you tend to come in for a lot of stick from the opposition.

I've even had injuries off my own team-mates at times. Ian St John and I were playing against Sunderland one year when we both went in to get the ball away from one of their players; there was a bit of a clash, and I ended up with three stitches in my mouth.

Now I've stopped playing and you could say football is going to leave me with a bad left leg (I don't know why because I really only use my left leg to walk and balance on, and it was my right leg, the kicking leg, on which I had the Baker's cyst operation), a disjointed toe, and my right ankle blown up out of proportion. This has happened through calcification of the bone, which occurs when fluid sets in on the ankle and doesn't go away, leaving you with an outsize joint. The only time it really hurts, though, is when I wear new shoes.

I have numerous scars on my legs and on my face, and I've got a couple of false teeth. I can't straighten or bend one of my left-hand fingers, and I've a weak wrist through playing on the American Astro-turf which doesn't give as much when you go down during a tackle. I have arthritis in both knees as well, so you could say I'm well worn. After some games in cold weather I can hardly move. I don't mean I'm lying there prostrate, but every movement is a bit of a chore.

Anybody going into football has to take for granted that at the end of the day, if he's at all successful, he's going to end up with this sort of legacy. However you play you're going to be left with some permanent reminders of your playing days. Your body is like a machine that's been designed to work for sixty years; all you're doing is working it twice as hard so that after thirty years it's knackered. Your parts just wear out.

Take Phil Boersma at Swansea now. Phil's no coward by any means and he's had his fair share of injuries. At the age of twenty-nine he broke his leg really badly. It could be the finish of his career – he's going to be out of the game for nine months, maybe a year. Every footballer must accept that it can happen to him – you just don't think about it all the time, or your game will suffer, but you have to make plans to cover the possibility.

That's why I get annoyed when people say footballers are paid too much. There can't be many 35-year-olds walking round with arthritis in both knees, a bad wrist, gashed shins, broken bones . . . I've paid for what I've got. It's all been hard earned.

As a youngster I could put on and take off weight quite easily. I still have the tendency to put on weight – Shanks called me 'Fatty' at one time, and that hurt, but these days I find I don't need to eat so much. I still take care of myself though. My ideal weight is around 13 stone. If I really diet I can get down to around 12 st 12 lbs, and I can play up to 13 st 7 lbs. My height is 5 ft 10¾ ins.

Weightwise, you get some players who never seem to put a pound on, yet they stuff themselves with ice-cream and drink lemonade every night. If I did that I'd shoot up to 18 st in no time.

Terry McDermott seems to exist on sandwiches and crisps. The night before a game you'll find him sitting in front of the telly, bags of crisps, plates of sandwiches, large glass of orange juice by his side . . . and he'll run it all off the next day.

Normally, on a Friday night before a game all I take is a laxative, and on Saturday morning I'll maybe eat a round of toast, and nothing more until the match is over.

Some players I know can eat baked beans before they play and run like they're jet-propelled. Everybody's different – I just stick to what I know is right for me. And I make up for it when the final whistle blows.

About five years ago I had trouble with my legs; that was when the specialist told me I had arthritic knees – it was something I would have to learn to live with. When I stopped playing they would probably give me a little bother, but for now the only thing to do was battle on.

Most footballers suffer from knee trouble. I have been luckier than most – I have never had cartilage trouble. But once when we were playing Setubal, the Portuguese side, one of their players went over the ball and clipped my knee. It was aching quite a lot so after the match I had it strapped up and went out for a meal with my wife Susie, and we ended up dancing, no problem. But about six the next morning I woke in agony. It felt like I'd never had such a bad injury before.

So I went down to Anfield early and said to Bob Paisley, who can diagnose an injury as accurately as any specialist, 'My leg's killing me.' He recognized I'd done something really bad and gave me a crutch as soon as he saw me, before he even looked at it. Then he told me he thought I'd broken it, so I went up to the hospital, had it X-rayed and was then told the side of my kneecap had been chipped off.

I was told I'd been lucky. A blow like that could have shattered my kneecap, but only the side of it had come away in the collision. If I'd had an office job they would just have left it and let it heal itself in three or four weeks, but as I would be running on it in the future, they decided it would have to come out.

So I went into Broadgreen Hospital and was in there maybe a week before they operated. And when they gave me the piece of bone, about the size of a half-crown, I was amazed.

I was very frustrated lying in hospital – I'm not the world's most perfect patient – and it always seemed quite embarrassing to me to have to use a bedpan. I got quite stubborn about it, and said I wouldn't eat, until they agreed I could get out of bed and hobble to the toilet.

I remember I was in a private room at the top of the ward, and the door would often be left ajar so I could see the line of three or four beds at the end. One morning there was this good-looking cadet nurse walking down the ward with a bedpan in her hands and a brave face on, smiling at the patients as she went by, but as soon as she passed the last bed, she lifted her eyes to heaven and mouthed a silent 'Urrgh!' It must have been terrible – and I thought then I'm not going to embarrass some young bird like that.

So the doctor told me I could get up, and I went down to the toilets on my crutches. Only trouble was the leg was in such a stiff splint, when I did sit down I ended up with my leg near the top of the door! I got back to my bed in a cold sweat.

After that I kept on until they let me go home – but they said, 'Be sure to keep the splint on and come back and see us in a

ABOVE LEFT Tommy the lad – 'never deliberately naughty'.

ABOVE His father Matty, who died when Tom was in his teens.

His mother Margaret – 'she's still the boss'.

Tommy's first game at Anfield was with his school youth team (Under-11s) in 1956. He's the third lad from the left in the back row.

Groundstaff days – forking the pitch with Phil Tinney and Bobby Graham.

Bringing the FA Cup home to Liverpool for the first time in 1965 – Ron Yeats holds it aloft at the Town Hall. Tommy Smith is to the left.

Liverpool FC, 1966 vintage – skipper Ron Yeats presents Ian Callaghan with his Young Player of the Year award. *Back row (left to right):* Gerry Byrne, Tommy Lawrence, Chris Lawler, Roger Hunt, Gordon Milne. *Front row:* Tommy Smith, Phil Thompson, Willie Stevenson and Ian St John.

On tour with England Under-23s to Czechoslovakia, West Germany and Austria in 1966. Tommy *(foreground)* shares a joke with Nobby Stiles. *Background:* Peter Bonetti, Gordon West, Bobby Tamblin, Paul Reaney, George Armstrong and Alf Ramsay.

Pre-season training – Peter Cormack, Kevin Keegan, Terry McDermott take it seriously, but at least Tommy, Roy Evans and Jimmy Case can manage a smile.

Ronnie Moran eases the pain during a clash with Sheffield United, while Ian Callaghan looks concerned.

More typically – Tommy dishing it out, this time against Norwich.

'Without a doubt he was the greatest influence on my career' – Bill Shankly hands Tommy his Inside Football Player of the Year Trophy the day before Liverpool met Arsenal in the FA Cup Final, 1971.

Scourged by referees – sent off by Clive Thomas, Maine Road, in February 1973.

One of the best matches ever seen in America – Tommy tackles Pele in Tampa Bay Rowdies' clash with New York Cosmos, 1976.

The best dressed side in the League, in the 1970s. *Back row:* Ray Kennedy, Phil Neal, Jimmy Case, John Toshack, Ray Clemence, Terry McDermott, Steve Heighway, Brian Hall, Peter Cormack. *Front Row:* Tommy, Emlyn Hughes, Ian Callaghan, David Fairclough, Phil Thompson.

The goal that sealed a legend – Tommy scores with his head in Rome against Borussia Moenchengladbach in the European Cup Final, 1977.

Tommy celebrates victory in Rome with Ronnie Moran.

To the victor, the spoils – the morning after the Rome final.

Tommy at the Palace, receiving his MBE awarded in the Jubilee Honours List, alongside rugby star J.P.R. Williams and tennis ace Roger Taylor.

Liverpool manager Bob Paisley leads Kevin Keegan and Tommy Smith into a disciplinary hearing at the FA headquarters in Lancaster Gate.

Tommy in the dugout at Anfield with Joe Fagan in November 1979.

Where it all began – Tommy outside 9 Lambeth Road, Liverpool, his childhood home.

The battle he lost – Tommy built a six-foot wall around his new home in Crosby, Liverpool to deter Sunday sightseers, but after a long wrangle with the council was forced to take it down. He's now growing a nine-foot hedge.

Tommy and his family today – wife Sue, daughter Janette and son Darren.

week.' When my mate Wilf Preston came to fetch me I was waiting at the hospital gate for him I was so determined to get away – he didn't even have to carry my bags. And I took the splint off in the car to get myself more comfortable. When I got home I started doing exercises with the leg – it didn't seem to do any harm. Each time I went back to the hospital, I'd put the splint back on and they'd say, 'Yes, it's doing all right, coming along nicely . . .'

It was the worst injury I ever had. It took me nine weeks to play again, almost as long as the time when I pulled my thigh muscle in a game against Spurs. That time I was trying to get fit and Shanks caught me in the medical room at Anfield with Joe Fagan shaving my leg preparatory to strapping it up. Shanks said, 'What the hell are you doing?'

I said, 'I want to play, so Joe's strapping my leg.'

He said, 'Don't be daft. You're not playing. Get off that table!'

After a bit of an argument, I said, 'I am playing. It's my leg.'

Straight away he answers back, 'It's not your bloody leg. It's Liverpool FC's leg! And you're not bloody playing!'

In fact I did play in one or two games – with a strapping on and wearing a pair of slightly longer shorts to hide the bandage.

Another time I had a really bad injury was when we were playing the Swiss side Servette in a European Cup-tie at Anfield. I tackled a fellow at the Anfield Road end – he'd gone round Chris Lawler, and I slid in to stop him. As I tackled him, he went over the ball, and I knew he'd done something to me, so I whacked him with my arm for good measure.

I got up and walked away, but as I reached the middle of the pitch I thought 'My leg feels a bit numb,' so I looked down and my stocking was all torn. When I rolled it down there was a cut that began half-way up my shin and ran right down almost to the ankle. And it was just, well, open. I could see the bone, and the tissues and everything.

So I sat down on the pitch and called for Joe Fagan. It was the last minutes of the game – we were going to win anyway so I walked off to the treatment room.

I was lying there, and the Anfield medic Dr John Reid came

in and said, 'That's the worst cut I've ever seen' – immediately making me feel terrific. But it was a clean cut, there was no blood or anything.

And then his brother, Dr Bill Reid, comes in, takes a look and says, 'Oh well, while you're lying there doing nothing, sign these two autograph books.' While I'm lying there and they're deciding what to do, Dr John says, 'First off get him a large Scotch, and while you're at it get me one as well – and put some dry ginger in it.'

I lay there thinking, 'I don't believe this. . . .'

Then Dr John says to me, 'It's a good job I brought some extra stitches with me.' Turns out he's brought only six, and when he tries to stitch it up it keeps coming apart again. He pulls a stitch, and the cut snaps open. 'Do us a favour,' he says, 'push it together.' I'm lying on the table, pushing this cut together while he stitches it, and he turns round and says to Joe Fagan, 'Joe, come here and put your thumb on that knot. . . .'

He somehow manages to close it up with the six stitches, and fills the cut with a cleansing powder. 'You'll be all right,' he says. 'It's going to pain a bit tomorrow, so here's a prescription. You're bound to have a bit of poison in it after all that messing around.'

The following morning I'm lying in bed, afraid to put my foot to the ground, and when I do eventually decide to get up, the blood rushes to my leg and the bandage gets all messy, and I'm feeling pretty rough.

Susie goes to get the post. A couple of weeks before, I'd done a publicity thing for the *Sun* newspaper with David Webb, of Chelsea, and Ian Ure, of Manchester United. We'd been photographed in some new Italian football kit that was on the market. So that morning the photographs arrived through the post, and I opened them up.

In one of them I was kneeling on one knee on the floor holding a football in front of me, but the way the photographer had taken it, it was plain I was showing one ball too many. We had such a laugh over that one I nearly broke my stitches open again, but it was just the tonic I needed to lift me that day. I didn't play again, though, for a good four weeks.

Many injuries are nothing more than a state of mind. With the adrenalin flowing, all you want to do is get on with the game, so the little things go by the board.

I know an awful lot of people who have played with injuries. If you let them bother you, you're going to get injured every week.

We were in Norway playing a friendly and I went to head a ball half-way through the second half and ended up heading it awkwardly because it dipped. I did something to myself and had to come off, but thought it was just a little muscle thing . . . this was on the Tuesday or Wednesday. That Saturday I played against Manchester United and Jimmy Greenhoff elbowed me early on, so I felt a bit sore. On Monday I went for an X-ray and found out I'd been walking round with a broken rib for the best part of a week. Ribs are definitely the most painful things to break. There's not a lot one can do except wait for them to heal, but while you're waiting every movement can be agony. A cough can make you feel like you're dying.

One day at Melwood training ground, during the first season we won the European Cup, I'd had a lot of trouble with my knee again, and I'd gone for exploratory tests. The specialist this time gave me a local anaesthetic and injected a dye in my leg before putting me under this machine, like an X-ray machine, where the dye would hopefully show up what was wrong. He found out I had a cyst at the back of my knee. It began the size of a pea, but grew to the size of a golf ball, and eventually it got to the stage where I couldn't straighten my leg and it had to come out. It was about Christmas time when I went into hospital for the operation, and while I was in there I decided to pack it in at the end of the season, have my testimonial and call it a day.

The operation itself came about in almost an offhand way. I was prepared for the theatre and there was a chap in the room next to mine who was in for a cartilage op. When they wheeled me down to the theatre they found out the surgeon had already started on him, so they wheeled me back to my room and I ended up going to sleep in front of the telly while I was waiting.

After the operation, because the anaesthetic tube had been in my mouth, I remember thinking they must have operated on my throat when I came round – I could hardly talk. And there were fifteen stitches in the back of my leg, all for a little cyst.

The day after the operation, one of the nurses came in – they were nuns, because this was Park House private nursing home in Liverpool – and she said 'I have to bath you.' I didn't fancy that so I kidded her the doctor had told me I could get up. I said, 'Do me a favour – get me a plastic bag and a couple of elastic bands, and I'll take a shower myself.'

Truthfully I had asked the doctor if it was all right to get up – he probably thought I wanted to go to the toilet or something, and he'd said yes. So I strapped the plastic bag over my knee, secured it with the elastic bands and went and had a shower.

Walking back to my bed, feeling all nice and fresh, I got copped by the Mother Superior, and she went crackers! She reacted like she'd seen a ghost. In the end they asked me to use a wheel-chair if I got up again.

I never have liked hospitals. After about a week I've had enough and want to get home.

I got injured pretty badly in a car crash just before Christmas 1972. We were returning from beating Spurs 2–1 at White Hart Lane and I'd had a bad stomach. Normally if we beat a London club we have a few beers on the train, but I'd been drinking milk because I felt under the weather. It didn't help much when we got into Lime Street Station and I went off for a quick visit to a friend, to come out and find someone nicking my car. A mate of mine who had a van went chasing after them with me in the passenger seat, and they headed out of Liverpool towards Preston.

We followed them for quite a way, till they turned on to the Ram's Head pub forecourt at Tarleton, jumped out and into another car. We gave up then – we were just happy to get mine back. I checked my car was all right, my mate drove off and I started off for home.

Now I was well out in the country by now, north of Burscough, and in those days I lived near Ormskirk, so I had to go back through these quiet lanes to get there. And on one of these lanes I hit a patch of black ice, the car spun round and I ended up in the ditch.

I must have been concussed – I was certainly very lucky because the windscreen ended up in the back seat, but I wasn't cut about. I don't remember doing it but I must have tried to get the car out of the ditch, for when my mate came to move it next day he found bricks under the wheels and deep tyre ruts where I'd been revving it up.

Next thing I remember is walking along the road to get help, and, because the car had ended up facing the other way to the one I was going, I ended up back at the pub crossroads. But I was so befuddled that instead of going into the pub I turned round and started walking back the way I'd come.

By then I felt a little better, though I did have a pain in my side, so I started jogging. I even tried to flag a police car down but he didn't stop. And the car couldn't be seen from the road because it was right down in this ditch. So I jogged on into Burscough before a taxi came by – I was standing by this telephone-box, trying to ring for one in fact – and stopped and took me home. It was about four in the morning and I guess I must have walked or jogged a good eight or nine miles.

I got to bed in a bit of a state and next morning the pain was so bad Susie insisted I must go to Ormskirk Hospital. As soon as I got there a fellow in reception recognized me and came over and slapped me on the shoulder – 'Hello, Smithy. How are you doing?' I could have murdered him – the pain was terrible.

In the X-ray they discovered I'd cracked four ribs and fractured my shoulder and the ribs had pushed my lung in a bit. They were afraid of a puncture, so Liverpool FC put me in Park House Hospital again and I stayed a week or more, for a bit of a rest, then took it easy around the house for a few weeks. It was four or five weeks before I played again.

But the reports and rumours that flew around after that crash were unbelievable. Because I was Tommy Smith, and had a certain reputation, people were sure I'd been drinking, and I was supposed to have had four birds in the car with me. It was a Volvo so I suppose that stopped me from getting any more serious injuries, but even if anybody else had been in the car there would have been bodies everywhere! Because it was getting near Christmas they said I must have been celebrating, when in truth I felt like death before I set out. I was talking to a pal who was chauffeur to Cecil Moores and he said the black ice was so bad around those lanes that night that he'd nearly come adrift near that same spot – which made me feel better.

7 The Bee in my Bonnet

There's no doubt about it – Bill Shankly's been the biggest influence on my career. As a manager Shanks ate, drank and slept football – he still does – and expected his players to do the same. He never seemed to have a break from it – he related everything to football. It seemed as if nothing else existed.

There was a day when we were playing Manchester United, and Reuben Bennett had been to see them play; we were in the players' lounge and Reuben was giving his report. Shanks said, 'Right, now we'll go through their team . . . goalkeeper Stepney, oh, he's bloody awful on crosses . . . right-back so and so, he's no good . . . left-back Dunn, he can't defend . . . right-half . . .' He went through the team until he reached inside-right or something . . . 'and him,' he says, 'he's the worst player in the world.' So Reuben casually says, 'You can say that again!'

Shanks heard that, and he started off, 'Well, there's the goalkeeper Stepney . . .' And he went through the whole lot again, he was so involved with what he was saying.

We used to have tactics meetings at Melwood, and Shanks would have the board set up with the two teams in Red and White. He always used to set the opposition out in Red; he had this superstition about the colour. The players would be set out on the board and the first thing he'd do was take the opposition forward line away – 'Boom, boom, boom, they're no good – now let them worry about us!'

Many's the time I've been there and he's started talking about the other side – 'Oh, the outside-right always likes to do this, and the inside-left always likes to do that, and you know about this fellow – he always comes inside and hits it with his left foot . . . ' and then out of the blue he'll sweep them all off the board and say, 'Never mind about them. Now this is what we ought to try and do.'

He was amazing; he would drum the basics into us, while letting players' natural ability and character shine through and dictate the way they played.

Take little things like throw-ins, for instance. Bill Shankly devised throw-ins that were never complicated, but were effective. A lot of teams struggle on basics like throw-ins, but not Liverpool – they just do it simply, naturally.

Shanks always taught us there was nothing wrong in using the goalkeeper too. A lot of people think the goalkeeper is there solely to stop the ball going into the net, but the team is made up of eleven men. There's nothing wrong with pushing the ball back to the goalkeeper, who throws it out to a defender.

Shanks worked out the 4–4–2 scheme which we used effectively. The only time things ever broke down was when people forgot about the basics, and let them go by the board.

I'm always ready to praise what Shanks did for Liverpool, but I also gave him stick in my time. I think my biggest disappointment was getting dropped from the first team, especially the way he did it. Looking back on it, though, he probably did me a big favour.

It wasn't until I'd been dropped and started to think about leaving Liverpool that I began to realize there were other things in the world besides Liverpool FC. Since I was a kid I'd supported the club, and to captain them was a greater honour to me than to captain the England Under-23s. The biggest thrill in football was always to pull on a red Liverpool shirt on a Saturday.

I'd always been cocky, always confident, and this was something Liverpool and Shanks drummed into me as well. 'You are Liverpool FC, you are the top side, you are going to beat them in the tackle, you are going to score goals against them, you're not going to let anything in . . . '

It was going against everything I knew; the one thing Shanks forgot to teach me was how to accept being dropped. Suddenly, from being very aggresive, I had time to sit down for maybe the first time and think things out with my wife Sue. I was captain, and I had a lot on my plate – I used to organize the players' pool, I used to do a lot of things that maybe I should have shared around. It's not that I didn't trust anybody. It's just that I thought I was so capable I could do it. After a while I decided to start delegating things, and relaxing a bit, and my game picked up from then on.

Shanks and Liverpool FC also gave me confidence. They taught me to stand on my own feet – because I was an only child that wasn't too easy either.

I suppose that only since I started coaching have I fully realized that you have to be fair to everybody, you have to spread your emotions around, that it isn't good to concentrate on one player as the rest of the squad will suffer. In short, you have to be ruthless sometimes for the sake of the team. But I didn't know that at the time, and it hurt.

Shanks was the driving force behind the changes at Anfield. He came in like a tornado – I believe if he'd have got hold of a bulldozer he'd have flattened the ground and started again, rebuilding Anfield like he rebuilt the team. They built the new Kemlyn Road stand during his time and refurbished the Kop to a certain extent. They also built the new Anfield Road stand.

He was a great one for organization. And he got everyone on their toes. You didn't have to worry about whether the pitch was going to be all right, whether your boots were going to be there, who was going to look after the travelling . . . Shanks had it all worked out.

When we used to go away with the side he'd even decide what we could eat. The meals would invariably be a drop of tomato soup, a steak, fresh fruit and cream followed by tea and toast. It seldom varied. Shanks was never one to wait for service. If the waiters didn't appear quickly he'd be off into the kitchens saying, 'Look, these lads want feeding – see to it.'

It wasn't for a long time, till lads like Steve Heighway joined the club and started questioning one or two things, that Shanks began to realize maybe everybody didn't like steak or tomato soup, and we used to have a few choices. Perhaps one lad would have fish, another chicken, but it took time.

There was a time, when Steve first came, when we were playing Burnley the first game of the season and we'd gone to stay just outside Burnley. The usual drill was tea and toast and then to bed. We were trooping through the hotel reception when we found Stevie ordering chicken sandwiches and coffee – we couldn't believe it. It hadn't happened before.

Chris Lawler and I got into trouble with Shanks once over our favourite food. When we played Celtic in the semi-final of the Cup Winners' Cup we noticed black puddings on the hotel's breakfast menu. So we rang down to reception and asked if we could have black puddings for breakfast. The desk said no, they were all part of the mixed grill. To avoid messing about we ordered two mixed grills for the next morning – just to eat the black puddings.

Anyway about eleven o'clock that night we were in bed reading when Shanks burst in. 'Here, you two bums, what's going on?' He'd been checking through the breakfast orders and come across these two mixed grills. We tried to explain but he wasn't listening. 'You're not bloody having it,' he said, and stormed out. And we didn't.

Shanks knew how to lift the team, knew how to psyche you up. He knew the right things to say to the visiting team too – he'd go and greet them when they arrived at Anfield, then he'd come back and tell you, 'Christ, they look terrible today. They look like they've been out on the ale for a week . . .'

The psyching would begin at the Friday meeting, when we'd gather to talk about the coming match, and Shanks would say, 'They're coming here tomorrow expecting to get beat 2–0, 3–0 at the outside . . . let's make it five!'

At Liverpool FC they had things so organized that your kit would be out and ready for you when you arrived at the ground. All you had to do was get changed and play. They didn't let you worry about anything and they took as much pressure off you as they could.

When Notts Forest signed Trevor Francis in a blaze of glory, and Wolves signed Andy Gray with a fanfare, it put pressure on them to have a cracking first game, and gave them no chance to settle in.

Liverpool had Dalglish signed, sealed and delivered with the minimum of fuss, same with Souness, Ray Kennedy, Alan Kennedy . . . and straight away the lads can work their way in, settle down and play their own game.

Sometimes team selection could be a bit hazardous – and subject to Shanks's 'bathroom scenes'. Like if he wasn't too sure who should play in a certain position for that game you'd come in and maybe find two or three pairs of boots out where yours should be, and then it would be: 'Can I have a word with you, son?'

He'd take you into the bathroom and say, 'How do you feel?' And you say, 'Oh, I think I'll be all right.' 'Ah, but can you last the game?' 'Yes I think so . . . 'You were limping in training . . .' And he'd probably end up persuading you to rest.

Or it would be, 'How do you feel?' 'Oh, I'm struggling a bit.' 'How do you know? You looked all right in training yesterday. Have a go . . .' And you were in.

I remember Joey Jones turning up for one game, and he wasn't too sure about his leg, so he said to Joey, 'How do you feel?' and Joey says 'Oh, all right, I'll be okay.' 'I don't know,' says the boss, 'Maybe you'd better rest that leg today. It might be just as well . . .'

Then five minutes later Alan Lindsey turns up with stomach ache, so the boss has to go back to Joey and start all over again and convince him that maybe he's all right to play after all, having already persuaded him that he needed a rest!

Sometimes it would backfire on you though. I had a bad ankle but Shanks persuaded me to play one Saturday. We got beat and after the match he looked disgusted with me. 'You,' he said, 'you must have been the only captain in the Football League today who limped out to toss-up!' Yet he'd persuaded me I was fit!

Shanks tried to sign a full-back from Huddersfield at one time. He'd seen him play and brought him down to Anfield and told him, 'You're coming to the best club in the world, laddie. We have the best players, the best fans, the best facilities . . .' So the player says, 'Well, I've had offers from elsewhere. I'd like to consider.' Shanks says, 'Yes, well, take your time, but you'll do no better than coming here.'

A couple of days later the player telephones him and says, 'I'm awfully sorry. I'm going to join Arsenal.' And Shanks straight away down the telephone says to him, 'Ah, you were never any bloody good anyway. I didn't want you really . . .'

I had a love-hate relationship with Shanks if you like. One minute he could be the biggest so-and-so, the next day it was all forgotten and he was the nicest fellow you ever met in your life.

He was a fair man – he never cheated anybody. We only came to loggerheads once over money, and that was over a new bonus scheme they wanted to introduce. I never had to ask for a wage rise once while I was at Anfield.

But this year we'd won the Cup and he called us in and said they were going to reorganize the pay structure. 'What do you think you're worth?' he asked me. Well, a wise man keeps his mouth shut over that sort of question – I mean, you've got to give them brains. They've probably got some figure worked out in the back of their minds, and if you're way over that figure you're likely to get the chop.

Anyway they worked out this bonus scheme at Liverpool. Trouble was, the basic was terrible, and you found yourself relying an awful lot on bonus. One thing they didn't have to give at Liverpool FC were incentives. It is a good club and fellows go out there on Saturdays and play their hearts out no matter what.

We got together with the lads and I went back and got it sorted out with Shanks, but not without a bit of shouting and bawling. He'd stand there with his hands on his hips and say, 'You, Smithy, you could start a riot in a cemetery.' It was a good clean fight, though; it never came to a rift or anything and it was all sorted out.

Shanks's heart was always in the right place. At my testimonial he came up and gave me a cheque. He didn't have to and I refused it a couple of times, but he insisted and eventually gave it to Susie. I had to take it in the end, not necessarily because I needed it but because it would have hurt him if I hadn't.

Sometimes he did the most outrageous things. I was invited by my bank manager to a Rotary lunch at Liverpool's Adelphi Hotel when Shanks was the speaker, and he turned up with his wife Nessie, who's the sweetest person. Shanks started his talk, and he knew I was there, so before long he veered off his subject and started talking about me, saying in effect the biggest mistake I ever made was walking out on him at Arsenal, and that the incident probably cost me the captaincy of Liverpool. That was the first time he'd come out and said it just like that. Talking to him about it after the Arsenal game, he'd agreed with what I'd done and said if he'd been in my shoes he would probably have done the same thing. But some time later he was telling everyone it cost me the captaincy.

It was just one of those little things that bugged me about Shanks. Whether it had been preying on his mind or not I don't know, but it wasn't what he told me at the time.

In the weeks leading up to that Arsenal game we'd played at Leeds and got beaten 1–0, probably picked up only two or three away points, and Shanks wanted to know the reason why. He got me into his office and went through the side, saying Clem was off-form, Chris Lawler wouldn't hurt a fly, Alec Lindsay was no good, Hughsie was terrible, Steve Heighway was . . . about the only one he had praise for was Larry Lloyd, but he never really mentioned me.

Then came the Thursday and I guessed he was dropping me, because they play a practice game on the Thursday and if you're not in that you know the chances are you're not playing on Saturday. I felt like I'd been kicked in the teeth.

But he didn't have the guts to tell me straight out. I said, 'If I'm not playing I don't want to go to Highbury. I'd rather play in the reserves.' But he said I would be going and from then on it became a straight confrontation between him and me.

It was clear he was the boss and I was going to do what I was told. I'd argued with him before, but never questioned his authority. There was never a confrontation like now. He said he hadn't picked the team. I said, 'I know you've picked the team. Why try to make a fool out of me?'

I chatted with Peter Cormack when we got to London. He was also in the squad of fourteen. I said I wasn't playing and he said, 'Looks like I'm not playing either.' So I said, 'Well, I don't know what you're going to do. I'm not influencing you, but I'm away home.'

I didn't leave my bag on the bus like I usually do but took it in with me. They went through the team and when they got to 'Peter Cormack is twelfth man' I knew I was left out in the cold. So I said to Joe Fagan, 'All right then, I'll see you for training tomorrow,' picked up my bag and left.

I was coming out of the ground and there was a young lad, about thirteen or fourteen, and he said to me, 'Where are you going?' So I said, 'I'm not playing, I'm going home.' 'If you're not playing,' he said, 'then I don't want to watch. I'll come home with you.' That was probably the best compliment I'd ever been paid, certainly the nicest thing anybody had said to me for weeks. But I said, 'Don't be silly, son. You watch the game . . .' And I caught the tube to Euston and was back in Liverpool before five.

On the Monday Shanks called me in and after a chat told me he would probably have done the same thing. Then we discussed my future, and I decided I wanted to get away from Shanks and LFC. I was twenty-eight and I knew I could still play a bit.

It was probably very foolish, because the next thing I knew I was sitting in a friend's house when I heard a rumour I might be going to Stoke. Thinking about it then, I didn't really want to go anywhere – I even thought about packing the game in instead of moving on. All I really wanted to do was play for Liverpool.

Tony Waddington, who was then Stoke's manager, had arranged with Shanks for me to go on loan, but Shanks didn't tell me when. I was at Melwood training one morning and half-way through he came up and said, 'What are you doing here? You're supposed to be in Stoke by twelve.' So I said, 'Well, I'd appreciate a phone call or a tap on the shoulder next time.' I was fuming. Melwood groundsman Eli Wass gave me a lift home and by the time I got down to Stoke I was a good two hours late.

I was supposed to go on a month's loan and when the papers were drawn up Shanks refused to sign them, saying he wanted me back at five minutes' notice. The League wouldn't allow it so the deal fell through.

But the whole episode taught me a lot. I decided that if I were to play for Liverpool in the future, I'd play for myself. What I didn't realize was that Emlyn had already been canvassing for the captaincy.

However, I did go down to Stoke for a while, met the lads, began to realize there were other teams in the world besides Liverpool, and it opened my eyes in a lot of ways. The first thing I noticed was that they took their own kit home to wash it, and things like that. We never had to do that at Liverpool. The Stoke lads used to go for a bite to eat at the Supporters' Club, or at a little café next door; in fact they did pretty much as they pleased. Liverpool, on the other hand, was ruled by a code of discipline that never varied.

As it turned out, Chris Lawler got injured against Crystal Palace (he did a cartilage) and Shanks asked me to come back and play full-back in the first team, although he couldn't give me the captaincy back.

'I don't want the captaincy back,' I told him. 'That's your problem now, not mine. I don't mind playing but I'm going to play for me now – I'm not playing for you any more.'

So Shanks made Emlyn Hughes captain.

8 Codes, Moods and Feuds

Liverpool, like most football clubs, was ruled by a code of discipline – but it was a code founded on success and pride of playing for Liverpool FC. It was all based on common sense.

You need hard-and-fast rules only if you're losing – over the years we'd been winning quite consistently so there were never any problems. Generally we felt on top of the world, and this feeling was enough to carry us through the times when we did get beaten.

It's a measure of what the players felt for the club to reflect that I can recall no one being consistently late for training. Ian Callaghan might turn up at 9.30 for the 10 am session and still be putting his boots on at two minutes to ten. Someone else may come in at 9.55 and still be changed and ready for ten, but no one was really late. No player would consistently indulge in hanky-panky the night before a match, like going out and getting stoned on the Friday. When we went away we generally knew how to behave – Liverpool FC were welcomed and never banned from any of the hotels we used.

You have to give Shanks credit for this – he treated his players like grown men and not schoolkids. You couldn't imagine him insisting someone like Ron Yeats had to be in bed by ten or something, but he picked responsible players who knew the score, and he didn't mind them enjoying themselves, so long as they did it by the book.

Generally I suppose you could do what you liked so long as you didn't tarnish Liverpool FC's name and knew the limit of what would be tolerated.

It's got to be quite a tradition now that Liverpool don't have to crack the big whip – players on the whole respect and admire the club system.

That's not to say we didn't try it on now and again – just for devilment. I well remember playing Chelsea in London one time and being beaten. We were staying in a hotel down in Golders Green, and after the match all we wanted to do was drown our sorrows. Shanks had told us he didn't want us going out but none of us fancied drinking in the hotel with him watching us.

So we ordered a taxi, hoping to sneak out for a few pints. But as the taxi drew up in the hotel drive and we were creeping out, we met Shanks, Reuben Bennett and Bob Paisley coming back from a walk. And he says, 'Who's taxi is that?' So we say, 'Oh, not ours, boss. We're just going out for a breath of fresh air.' And there's the taxi driver saying, 'Of course it's yours and you owe me for coming out here!'

Anyway Shanks tells the taxi to leave and by then there were several of us hiding in the bushes like schoolkids, trying to attract the driver's attention to wait for us down the road till Shanks had gone in. . . . Eventually we all piled in and went out for a drink.

I think Shanks realized we were all dying to go out for a drink and probably went for a walk to give us a chance to escape. But having come back and caught us out he then had to pretend to be annoyed. He probably thought, 'Christ, can't they even sneak out without getting copped! This isn't their day at all. . . .'

Mind you, that's not to say he couldn't be genuinely annoyed when the occasion demanded.

We used to go to Blackpool now and again in the close season, or during the season for a break. Shanks always had visions of pepping us up and doing great things, so he used to send us to Norbreck Hydro.

We used to go to Blackpool purely and solely for the fresh air. At one stage we'd go straight after the game on the Saturday, which was a bit tough on our wives and families. Then we'd maybe have a relaxing night out with the lads, have a lazy day on the Sunday, maybe go out again in the evening, then on Monday have a game of golf or a sauna. If Shanks came up we'd have a five-a-side in the grounds of the Hydro, and maybe even on Tuesday morning before we went home.

Later on Shanks realized we were going out on the Saturday nights and relaxing too well. He'd come up mid-morning on the Sunday and some of the lads would still be in bed. So we started going up to Blackpool on Sunday mornings instead, and he'd stick around with us, have a meal and not go home till seven or eight at night.

I remember the first time we went we beat Sunderland about 5–1, so Shanks said, 'That did you the world of good. We'll go back again next week.' So you'd have to tell your wife again that you'd be off to Blackpool, and that didn't go down too well in a lot of cases.

Next week we beat Blackpool quite convincingly, so Shanks says, 'Right, we're off again.' By the time we've done it a third time, every other fellow in the team is on the verge of getting a divorce, but you have to explain to your wife that it's all part of your job, and if the boss says go. . . .'

Anyway we got to a game with Fulham, and right after that we had to fly out to Hungary for a European Cup-tie. We were beaten 2–0 at Fulham, and were truly knackered, so all of a sudden it's 'bloody Blackpool!'

It was all right as long as we were winning, but as soon as we lost at Fulham Shanks was looking for a scapegoat. He couldn't just accept that we'd had a bad game, there had to be a reason. And if it wasn't 'that chicken we had in that restaurant the other night . . .' or 'those bloody boots – they're no good', then it was 'bloody Blackpool'!

Word had obviously been getting back to Shanks that we'd been fooling around at the Hydro, going out for devilment and a quick drink while his back was turned. So he went through the team one by one – 'You were out . . . you were out . . . ' and he turns to me, 'And you, you twenty-year-old . . . you were bloody out as well!'

There were no orgies or anything like that – it was just devilment. We did get to Blackpool again and we did still manage to sneak out for the odd drink some nights. If Shanks was on the door, guarding the lobby, we'd creep out the window and along the roof.

I got so used to doing this that one night I was out the window, and half-way across the roof when I saw all the rest of the lads walking out the front door. They saw me and burst out laughing. 'You daft git, he's not there tonight. He's gone home!' So I nearly broke my neck for nothing.

We were staying and playing in Belgium one time, and this night Chris Lawler and I had gone to a casino just opposite the hotel but the rest of the lads had gone down to the village for a drink after the game.

At twelve o'clock Shanks stormed into the casino and dragged us back to the hotel. We knew he was in a foul mood, and we were up in our rooms, looking down the road, when we heard the rest of them coming back . . . there was Gerry Byrne, Roger Hunt, Geoff Strong, Tommy Lawrence, Gordon Milne, all singing and kicking a few beer cans along, that sort of thing. There was a small playground in front of the hotel and they were mucking about on the swings.

We knew Shanks was waiting downstairs, so we tried to tell them to quieten it a bit, but they didn't pay any attention. Too far gone for that! It was about half-past one, and they came falling into the lobby, shouting and bawling, and Shanks was so flabbergasted he didn't know what to do or where to start, and of all people he picks on Cally.

'You, Callaghan . . .' he says, and you can see he's searching for the right thing to say. 'You . . . I'm going to tell your wife on you!' Everybody just collapsed.

But Bill Shankly's relation with the players was usually good – he could have his off-days like most of us, but I think our respect for Shanks was built mainly on his enthusiasm for the game and the common sense he practised, tempered to a large extent by his humour, both conscious and unconscious.

He was fond of calling meetings. If there was nothing else to do on an afternoon, he would suddenly say, 'We'll have a meeting.' So you'd rush your dinner, then stick around waiting for him to have his dinner and what always seemed like a slow bath, then he'd come in and set the men out on the table. Then he'd start on about the old players, Tom Finney and the like . . . once was great, twice wasn't so bad, but by the third time it started getting to you. . . .

Anyway, he used to get the lads in tucks. He used to swear he knew this Scottish player who only had one leg. He'd say, 'What a player! Used to be on the wing, and they'd give him the ball, and he'd clip these great passes into the box . . . can't just remember his name, but he was terrific. Used to save a fortune on footwear. He'd go to cobblers to get his boot soled and heeled, and get his stump heeled at the same time. . . .' That was Shanks all over.

Although Shanks would drum the basics into us, and tell us to keep it simple, we seldom practised things like set-pieces and free-kicks. This was demonstrated in a Charity Shield match we played against Manchester United one year, when we were awarded a free-kick just outside their box. And we had Gordon Milne lined up for the ball, Willie Stephenson on the ball, Roger Hunt too . . . and when the whistle went the first man jumps over it, the second man jumps over it, the third man jumps over it, and there's no one left to take the kick!

We had three players all steaming off in different directions, and they turned round, looked at each other as much as to say, 'Who was supposed to kick the ball, then ?' It looked so comical, but it was also dead embarrassing – all because we hadn't really worked it out.

We were always told to keep it simple. Shanks used to play in the five-a-sides with us and it was never anything complicated. Mind you, we had to watch him. We used to play with cricket stumps and arguments always developed as to whether the ball went in over the stumps or not.

Anyway, Shanks nips in and puts it between the sticks and claims it's a goal, and we all say, no, it was too high. So he turns to Chris Lawler and says, 'Was it in?' Chris says, 'No, it was over the sticks.'

'Ah, you . . .' says Shanks. 'You don't bloody say much, and when you do, you tell lies!'

Then there was the time shortly after Steve Heighway first joined and we were at a meeting with Shanks. Now Steve in those days was still an amateur player in his mind as well as having a university degree, and he would take offence pretty quickly. He's a great lad, terrific fellow, but I remember a time when Shanks called him out for not helping a team-mate in a situation where he could have helped.

Shanks said, 'Tell me, son, if your neighbour's house was on fire what would you do? Would you get a bucket of water and help him put it out, or would you watch it burn down?'

I don't know how everybody kept a straight face, because Stevie in his wisdom gets up and says, 'Well, all I can say is till you ask me a serious question, I can't answer. If you ask me silly questions, all you're going to get is silly answers. . . .' That knocked Shanks back on his heels and set the place rocking, I can tell you.

Shanks did the fixed-odds pools coupon every week, and one of the old Anfield lads, Andy, would take it down to the betting shop for him. Shanks would have maybe a couple of quid on so many results.

One week he came in and said, 'That's it, I've won. Go and collect my winnings, Andy.' And Andy said, 'What are you talking about? I've already been down to the betting shop and you haven't won.' Shanks didn't believe him and became quite het up. Together they checked the copy coupon. 'That's all right, that's all right, yes . . . what's this?' And he'd filled in a wrong number – maybe he'd meant to fill in game 20 but he in fact filled in game 21.

Shanks gave Andy stick for that. 'You should have noticed that,' he said. 'You should have realized there was no way that was going to be a draw.' If Andy had changed it, and it had been wrong, I dread to think what would have happened – in any event he couldn't win.

When Bill Shankly retired it was a real shock. The pressures on any manager are unbelievable, and I honestly believe the boss had had enough. At the time he was going he said his wife was ill, but I think he was in need of a rest. The sad part about his retirement was the petitions that were got up to get him selected for the board. There was so much noise made about it he had to say something – and, being Shanks, he said it quite strongly. But then, he was that sort of person – he'd rant and rave all day but still be the best fellow you ever met.

The pressures you get managing a football team, or even just playing football, are not only the visible pressures of the game – they're hidden ones that a lot of people don't understand. For instance, the irate telephone calls in the night, the crank letters, the threats through the post . . . I've had them, Shanks had them, every player's had them . . . the insults to your missus and the kids; you've got to learn to live with them, but you never like them. You get lots of praise and people patting you on the back when you're doing well, but it never makes up for somebody coming round and calling your missus an idiot or getting at your kids. It doesn't make up for waking in the early hours of the morning with some stupid sod on the other end of the telephone, or for having to change your number every so often. There comes a time when you've had enough, and I think Shanks had reached that point long before he decided to retire.

He may not have realized what a hurdle it is to become a director after being a manager. A football club is really three clubs in one – you've got the players, the manager and his training staff, and the directors. They all have different functions and interests and they're all required to act differently.

I know when a player stops playing and goes into management the transition is enormous. One minute you're the friend of twenty-odd players, going out drinking with them, sharing jokes with them, the next you've got some half a dozen friends on the staff. Suddenly you're no longer part of the players' 'club' because they have things they want to keep from the boss, and you've got the responsibilities that keep you aloof from them. To become a director is to move up into a different world again, with all the responsibilities for the business of the club.

I still say anyone who comes into contact with Bill Shankly

comes out a better person. You might not like him, you might think he's a bloody nuisance, he might even bore you talking nothing but football, but his motivation is beyond question and his confidence unbelievable. It's his biggest asset. The trouble when he retired was that he couldn't change his attitude, couldn't settle down and keep his views to himself – so perhaps that's why he isn't a director today. He's not crafty, and would never dream of scheming his way on to the board. I can see him saying, 'They've got to take me as I am, or not at all. I've been shouting for years – why should I stop now?' He always gave the impression that he should have been made Lord Mayor of Liverpool at least; and why not (but then again, that's my opinion)!

You could say Shanks taught me too well if you like. He always taught me to look after myself. When I was captain, I always put the lads first and never pushed myself forward.

But after the Stoke incident even I started looking at Shanks in a different light – he'd always insisted you be your own man, then when I started showing it by standing up to him, he appeared to act surprised.

At twenty-eight my whole football career exploded and it could have been the end if I'd let it. I could have left Liverpool in a fit of pique – but I didn't want to play for anyone else. So I stayed and I found there were other more important things outside of football – my family and my business affairs among them.

I still see Shanks, I still speak to him. I'm grateful for all he taught me. All the lessons I ever learnt from Shanks boil down to confidence, bags of confidence, and coming to admire the man for what he is – he doesn't ask any more than that.

I suppose what really bugged me was the thought that I'd pulled my tripe out for Liverpool since I was a kid of fifteen, and from being Shanks's protégé he'd turned on me. Suddenly from being Shanks's boy – 'This is Tommy, watch your legs, don't get too near him, he'll bite you!' – suddenly from all that I decided to live a bit for myself. If I didn't want to be aggressive on the pitch, I didn't have to. Now the captaincy had been lifted off me I was going to play my own game, do my own thing. I wasn't going to do anything Shanks's way any more – I was going to do it my way.

Looking back on my ups and downs with Bill Shankly, I guess he never really wanted me to leave Liverpool. He probably didn't relish the thought of playing Stoke with me in their line-up, like a spy in the enemy camp. That's what I think anyway – and Shanks gave me the confidence to think that way.

Shanks probably didn't want to be made to look a fool, but what I couldn't stomach over the Stoke episode was his attitude – one minute I was his blue-eyed boy, the next he's treating me like the enemy. The whole incident left a cloud over Anfield for a while, but I honestly think Shanks did me a favour which I didn't appreciate at the time. My game improved when I shed the responsibilities of the captaincy, and so long as I was in the side, and we were still winning things, I didn't really care about anything else.

There was a time, around the same month as the Stoke deal was suggested, when we were at a meeting, and Shanks, if he hadn't picked his team, would just call out the numbers: 'no. 4 will do this, no. 2 that . . .' But that day he picked up the no. 4 marker and said, 'Tommy will do – ' And I said, 'Hold on a minute. Tommy's doing nothing.'

So Shanks said, 'What do you mean?' and I said, 'I'm not playing.' Shanks said, 'You'll have to play. I've given the team to the papers.' So I said, 'Well, you'll have to tell them I'm not playing, like you did last week and the week before.'

So Shanks said, 'You've got to play.' I said, 'You haven't asked me to play, pal. I'm injured – I've got a bad ankle . . .' Just after that Joe Fagan took me outside and said, 'What's all this about? What's the matter with you?' I said, 'I've got a cob on. I can be as stubborn as him when I want to be.' So he grinned and said, 'Have you really got a bad ankle?' I said, 'Yes and no . . . it's not bad enough not to play.' So he said, 'Are you going to play?' And I said, 'I'll play for you, Joe. I'm not playing for him this time.'

But then Joe Fagan often was the authority. Shanks and Paisley may have earned respect, but Joe had the knack to get the best out of you. Like in later years when David Johnson joined Liverpool and he wasn't training right, Joe had a go at him about his lack of concentration. Johnson answered him back, told him to go away. Joe turned on him and barked, 'Answer me back like that again, and I'll knock your head off.' Johnson was left in no doubt that he meant it too.

Joe's probably a bit hard to get to know when you first join the club. Even Ray Kennedy wasn't too sure about Joe at first, and he asked me about it. I told him, 'Joe's all right. It just his way. It's as simple as that!'

9 A Man of Many Faces

I enjoyed being captain of Liverpool. I enjoyed winning the League Championship with Liverpool while I was captain, and I was the first captain of Liverpool ever to win a European competition. But it got to the point where I'd taken too much on. I was so stuck into it, doing different things – public relations work for Liverpool and so on – that I really had two full-time jobs. When it was lifted off my shoulders I felt relieved. Stevie Heighway started to run the players' pool and I just played, which was great.

If I thought for one minute that people stopped respecting me because I had stopped being captain, I'd have left the place in a flash. But I knew, and Shanks knew, and – I think – the crowd knew, that they were getting the best of both worlds.

I never used the captaincy to get me anywhere but because I was captain I had to do a lot of things I didn't particularly want to do, such as attend banquets. There was one at Preston one year, when all four Lancashire sides had won all four divisions – Liverpool the First, Burnley the Second, Bolton the Third and Southport the Fourth. Shanks cried off going to the reception at the last minute so I had to do it. There were others as well, and it got to a stage where public relations were becoming a bit of a pain.

I'd always been a responsible person, but when I became captain I had to learn to share it round a bit. If we hadn't reached the Cup final in 1971 things might have been better, but because of it I took it on myself to negotiate everything – and I think the final and my game suffered for it.

It wasn't that I didn't trust anybody else, it was just that I thought nobody else knew how to do it. All I was doing in fact was laying myself open to criticism.

But we had a lot of young players then and Shanks said we had to consolidate, not let in too many goals, work on what we had . . . truthfully I worried myself sick about the team.

When I took over from Ron Yeats I developed a mother-hen complex which was no bad thing, I suppose. It just went along with the extra authority gained from doing the job. Up to then, if I'd gone to someone and wagged my finger at them I'd probably have been told to sod off. But being captain meant something; I'd wag my finger and get results. Even the crowd would sense it and say, 'Oh look, see how he's taking care of his lads out there. . . .'

One time, though, taking care of the lads got me sent off. We were playing Manchester City and I was protecting Phil Thompson, still only a young lad then, from Tommy Booth. I dragged Tommy off Phil, and then had a go at referee Clive Thomas for not stepping in and doing it himself. Probably I was in the wrong, but I must have thought at that moment that being captain gave me authority to tell the referee off. Anyway, he sent me off the field.

Mind you, I used my 'iron man' reputation to good effect while I was captain, and I know the lads respected me for it. It gave me great satisfaction in later seasons to know at the back of my mind that the players still respected me a lot more than they respected Emlyn Hughes. He didn't have the loyalty of the other players.

So Emlyn canvassed for the captain's shirt and got it. He did all right, and still is I suppose. That's the problem: Emlyn takes care of number one. This was demonstrated in 1976 when a circular came round from the FA asking us to form a committee within the club to discuss the prevention of dirty play and that kind of thing. Liverpool decided they would have the chairman, John Smith, to speak for the board, Bob Paisley to act as go-between for the management, and reserve team trainer Roy Evans, because it would be useful for the reserves to have a voice on the discussion.

Then we had to pick three representatives of the playing staff. Straight away, Emlyn thought he should be on the committee, as captain, while the rest of us believed the three players should be elected to the committee on merit. So Emlyn went to play his usual game of cards while the other players organized a secret ballot.

Ronnie Moran added up the votes and the three that got elected were Steve Heighway, Ian Callaghan and myself. To my mind this underlined the way the players felt.

But Emlyn doesn't worry me any more, now he's been enjoying First Division football with Wolves. As he gets older, I think more people are beginning to realize what he's really like. . . . As far back as the time he first joined I remember an instance of this.

We'd played in Cologne and a couple of other places preseason, and the night before we came home Chris Lawler and I went out for a few drinks. Next morning we came down to breakfast with a tremendous thirst on and ordered a couple of the beautiful orange juices they served in the hotel, plus eggs and bacon and all the rest. We were waiting for our meal when Emlyn came in and sat down near the door with Davey Wilson, a lad LFC had recently bought from Preston. As soon as our waiter came in with our breakfast, Emlyn's up and dived in, pulled the fellow over and grabbed our food. I didn't see it but Chris nudged me and said, 'Aye, Emlyn's nicked our breakfast.' Well, I know in some ways I'm bad-mannered but there are ethics . . . and I'm not one to sit back and let things happen.

I went over to Emlyn and said, 'Did you order that?' He said, 'No.' So I said, 'Well, that's our breakfast.' He then pushed the half-eaten tray towards me and said, 'Well, you have it then.' To fully appreciate this, you have to know Emlyn's eating habits. When he is served with a meal, he'll immediately sort out what he doesn't want and shove it all on to a side plate, then proceed to eat what's left as fast as he can. So by the time I'd got to him that day, he'd swilled half that breakfast off the plate. Although

I'm not the most graceful eater in the world, it had reached the stage when I would try and eat at the other end of the room rather than watch Emlyn.

On this occasion I grabbed him and said, 'If you ever do that again I'll cut your bloody fingers off!' I got hold of Davey later on the coach and advised him not to follow Emlyn's pattern.

Another problem I had with Emlyn was that people would say I was jealous because he's been made captain of Liverpool. To a certain extent I resented him being captain, probably because he schemed it.

While I was captain I never went in to see Shanks just for the sake of it. We had constructive chats, but I was never one to see him for the sake of keeping in with the boss. I'm just not that way inclined.

One day in the dressing-room I confronted Emlyn with something he had done recently, and told him what I thought of him. What did Emlyn do? He said nothing because he knew I was in the right. Once I'd done it and got it off my chest, that was it. However, I still don't particularly like the chap and I'll never forgive him for almost screwing up my testimonial. You only get one once in your career and mine was nicely timed – we'd just won the European Cup and I'd been lucky enough to get that goal. Everything was going so well, and then Emlyn got up in front of half a million people outside the Walker Art Gallery and asked them to sing, 'Liverpool are magic, Everton are tragic.' Then we went inside, and he did it again, for which Bob Paisley apologized. A lot of my friends are Evertonians, whether you like it or not. If there was a war between Liverpool and Everton I'd be on Liverpool's side, but there isn't – just a football game. On the bus route from Liverpool airport, on our way back from Rome, there were plenty of people dressed in blue as well as red cheering us. It was a great occasion for the city, not just for the club. We'd won the League, we'd won the European Cup, we'd only just got beaten in the FA Cup, and my testimonial was the following Friday. Then Emlyn spoils it all.

People rang me up saying, 'Don't expect me to come to the game.' Emlyn went on television later to give some half-hearted apologies; it's crazy to think he worried me so much but for tuppence I would have knocked his head off. It took me all my time to contemplate even talking to the fellow. He's probably the only person I've met at Liverpool that I've never got on with, and you're talking about some hundred and fifty players. Football-wise, he's all right. They call him 'Crazy Horse' because he's got bags of energy. He has been part of Liverpool and you can't take that away from him.

I remember the first game of one season when we were playing QPR. On the pre-season tour I had filled in as captain for Emlyn who had been injured, but now he was back in the side as captain and I was on the bench, which I wasn't too happy about. We didn't play that well and we were a goal down at half-time; they scored another in the second half because we were by then in such disarray.

In the dressing-room afterwards Bob Paisley starts ranting at Emlyn – and remember everyone was feeling a bit sick at losing – and says, 'What the hell were you playing at? You were supposed to get them organized at the back. We were only getting beat 1–0. Come the end of the season and that extra goal they scored could make quite a bit of difference to us.' Now all the time I was captain there was no way I picked the team or demanded team changes, but I got an insight into Emlyn's methods that day because in the heat of the moment Bob let slip, 'You don't know what the hell you want. You've already been in to see me saying the team was slow at the back. . . .'

To my mind it was pretty obvious that Emlyn had been complaining that Alec Lindsay and I were slow. He's not exactly the fastest man on two feet himself. It took me a lot of concentration to change and get out of that dressing-room without sticking one on him.

Emlyn doesn't seem able to accept defeat or disappointment very well either. Sometimes you have to swallow your pride and go along with events for the good of the team.

There was another match towards the end of the season after Emlyn's testimonial, when Liverpool beat Villa to win the League. Emlyn was left out – he'd been dropped since Liverpool had been beaten by United in the Cup semi-final – but he turned up and sat in the trainers' box. I too was at the match and, although I was playing for Swansea, I still felt for the lads because I'm basically a Liverpudlian. Anyway, ten minutes before time, with Liverpool winning, Emlyn went home. I know if I don't play I'm not too happy, but I would show up to let the lads see I was happy for them.

You can't be emotional as a captain. You have to get over thinking you're Superman holding the team together, and that they'll crumble without you. They are going to go on winning – that's Liverpool's strength. But Emlyn can turn it on and off whenever he likes. He's a man of many faces. We get beaten in the Cup final and he's got the saddest dog face; we win the European Cup a few days later and he's got the biggest smile in the world. You have to be very stable as a captain, and be able to lift the team when they're down. Emlyn knew how to lift the players if, for example, the chairman walked in. One minute he'd be sitting there quietly, not saying a word, the next he'd be on his feet saying, 'Come on, lads! We've got to give 'em stick today! Let's have a good game. . . !

There was never any question that Emlyn wasn't a good player, though. His parents were super people, and his wife and children are terrific, but he tends to lead this Jekyll and Hyde existence. It's only him I occasionally felt like strangling – if he had half the character and charisma of his father he'd be a far better person.

I remember when Emlyn was left out of the side when Liverpool won the League title again – it was only because he was getting older. All players have to come to terms with that at some point and face up to no longer being an automatic first-team choice. I had to face disappointment when we met Bruges in the European Cup final at Wembley in 1978. I'd dropped a pick-axe on my foot and broken my toe shortly before the final. I was really sick at not being able to play. After the game I was stuck up in the television commentary box, filling in for Kevin Keegan, trying to tell the interviewer how happy I was for the lads, when all I wanted to do was get down on that pitch and join in the celebrations. I was so thrilled for them it was bloody frustrating to watch them leaping about without me.

Earlier that day, though, I had caught Joey Jones in a foul

mood and eventually got out of him that Emlyn had been having a go at me behind my back. The lads probably realized that if I found out there'd be hell to pay.

After the Bruges game there was a buffet reception for the winners. I hobbled over to Emlyn on my crutches and told him what I thought of him. Not content with that, he followed me back to my table. My wife Susie told him frankly, 'You'd better disappear before you get killed.'

I might have passed the time of day with him before that game, but since then I haven't spoken to the man. But you don't carry your grudges on to the park with you – when you're out there from 3.00 to 4.40 on a Saturday afternoon you're playing for LFC. Off the pitch, it's a different matter. Emlyn has ability and has achieved a lot, but at the same time he has, in my view, a bigger ego than any other man I've known.

10 Hard Nut, Soft Centre

This hard-man image of mine came about through a conscious decision I made when I was playing as a youngster. I figured out the only way to win was never to let the other fellow see you were beaten in any way. So I didn't shirk tackles and it seemed to work. I found people admired me more for getting stuck in, not necessarily kicking the other fellow, but tackling hard.

In a way it was an extension of when I was a kid, living in the surroundings I knew. If you wanted to get on you had to show a bit of edge; the harder you tried the better it seemed to get. A lot of people were jealous because they didn't quite make it as footballers, yet they were good enough to play in the same school team as me, or the same schoolboy side. They say they never quite got the breaks – what they didn't realize is, you've got to make the breaks. Instead of going to bed early on a Friday night before a game, they'd rather go out and have a beer. They didn't take the game seriously enough. There were a lot of better players than me knocking around when I was a kid, but they just didn't have the attitude to become professional footballers.

I often get asked when I speak at dinners, 'What did you say to Duncan McKenzie, or Joe Jordan, or Malcolm MacDonald . . .' The truth is, you don't have to say anything. I'd probably mutter the same threat to anybody I played against, 'I'm gonna break your effing back.' When I met Rodney Marsh in Tampa

Bay, he said that was the one thing he remembered about me when he played against me for the first time!

I even gave my wife Susie a fright on one occasion. She'd seen me play at Anfield scores of times, of course, but there the main stand is quite a way from the pitch. When she came to see me play at Swansea, where the main stand is almost on the touch-line, she was horrified! 'You looked absolutely wicked!' she said. 'Goodness knows what frights you must have given players at Anfield!'

People used to get disappointed if you didn't go out on the field and get stuck in. It got to the point where they'd look at me a bit funnily if I left out the tough-guy bit. It took me a long time to convince football writers I could play a bit as well! It's hard to change people's opinions though. Even today if people don't know me, they look as though they're expecting me to sock them on the nose any minute. It's all part of the legacy left over from the days when I was dubbed 'the Iron Man of Anfield', and I guess it's a tag I'll never lose.

The hard men are missing from the game today. A few years ago they outlawed the tackle from behind, which was quite right, but it seems to have knocked the physical side of the game on the head. Years ago you could look round any side – like Liverpool had Gerry Byrne and big Ron Yeats – and say they had people who could take care of themselves. I'm not saying the others couldn't but you at least had a mainstay of players who rarely shirked a tackle. At Leeds you had Bremner and Hunter; at Everton, Labone and Tommy Wright. You look round the leagues now and there are few names that spring to mind that the press can call 'assassins' like they used to.

Yet they can still be an essential part of any team. Taking them out of the game means English football now lacks a core of physical players who can throw out their chests and say, 'I'm going to win today, because I'm stronger than that bugger over there.'

At the time we won the World Cup you had players like Nobby Stiles and Jackie Charlton who could get stuck in but could also play. Other foreign sides still have their hard men, but England at the present moment don't seem to possess them like they used to.

Ronnie Harris is a good example of the hard man, the good honest pro who doesn't ask for anything, doesn't give anything. I got to know him well in the early days, but his style of football is on the way out sadly. All we're left with are the sneaky ones who get away with murder and the 'nearly' men who are no good to anyone. Joe Jordan we used to call 'Just Joe'; Derek Spense, of Blackpool, was another player like that. If they got paid for standing up in a game they'd be out of pocket, because they spent more time on their arse than they did on their feet. Time and again they'd 'just' fail to make the ball, 'just' fail to score . . . it might look good, but it means nothing.

I wasn't always as hard as I thought I was. If you were the new boy at the club, they'd bring you down to earth by making you the scapegoat for anything if you weren't careful – but it was all in fun.

Like at the post-match inquests they'd say, 'Right, who's missing today? Oh, so-and-so's just nipped to the toilet. Right, we'll blame him!'

One of my first games at Anfield was against Leeds. We had been beaten by them at Elland Road 4–2 that season, and when they came to Anfield, early on in the match they won a free kick just outside our penalty area. I lined up in the wall as Bobby Collins came up to take the kick, and then I moved . . . deadly sin! Tommy Lawrence managed to push the ball down but it got put into the back of the net by someone else. I got some stick for that, but then I scored the equalizer, which made up for it to a certain extent, and eventually Peter Thompson scored the winner.

Shanks used to slate us for things like that, though, and rightly so. He'd slate us for lack of effort – when we played Manchester United and got beat 3–0, nobody had a damp shirt, and he was talking about getting overcoats fitted for those people who'd been standing around most of the game. What made it worse was that we'd turned in this dismal performance shortly before we had to meet Leeds in the FA Cup final.

As I got older, things did settle down to a certain extent but now and again I had to pull a hard tackle out for the right occasion, or else people would think I was going soft.

On one occasion we were playing Manchester United, and up against Joe Jordan – he likes to go round doing what he likes. Well at Anfield I got stuck into him, only to prove that if he was going to do any rough stuff he'd picked the wrong person. So I picked him up and dusted him off, which made him look a bit of a fool.

I think if anyone wants to mix it on the pitch I can take care of myself. If ever I've forgotten myself or let things go by the board, I'm usually brought back to my senses by somebody whacking me from behind, and I realize what I should be doing. Not going round kicking people, but tackling and tackling hard. Once you've got their attention, and they're not concentrating on the ball you're the winner. You must concentrate on the game all the time. It's no good being worried about somebody at the back of you.

We played Ipswich at Anfield in May 1977, and Paul Mariner and I went for the ball. I think he got excited because he was playing against a supposedly hard man and he butted me. I had double vision for a while – must have looked as if I was glaring at him, but the truth was I couldn't see that well! Shortly after that Steve Heighway got involved in an incident with Mick Mills and was carried off with a head wound. All this happened in the first few minutes.

The next time the ball came I tackled Mariner really hard and gashed his shin. But only because I had stars in my eyes.

The referee came over and said, 'Go off for treatment,' but I said no, I didn't want to go off. It was an important game – we had a chance of winning the title. But one or two of us felt it that day because it was Ipswich's chance of closing the gap on us. They had to win, so they came intending to kick us to death. As it happened they were beaten 2–1 in the end.

In the second half it was quite funny, because there were two of them chasing a loose ball and I dived between them and came out with it – the two of them chickened out. I pushed it forward for Jimmy Case and the next minute it's in the back of their net.

There's no way, at least not too often, that a player is the same on the field as off. If people would only recognize that football is your job, and it's like the executive of some big company running things in the office all day, making big decisions and bawling people out to do this, do that . . . when he gets home you'll probably find his children can twist him round their little fingers.

It's the same with me. I'll not shirk anything on the pitch, but when I get home my children can wrap me round their little fingers as much as anybody else. If people could understand that footballers look on what they do as a job and not just a sport, they'd probably understand the game better too.

But then you do play to the gallery to a certain extent. We were playing Norwich at Carrow Road one time and I had to come off – I'd pulled a calf muscle – and as I'm walking round the ground with Ronnie Moran someone had a go at me from the crowd. I just stepped towards the terraces where he was standing and growled, then watched him jump. I burst out laughing. But if people want to see me do that they're not going to be satisfied with anything less.

There don't seem to be so many characters in the game these days. When I first started you could go to a match and be entertained, because the players weren't just footballers, they were characters too.

Take Liverpool, you had Ian St John, and Roger Hunt; you could go through the team and you'd find characters. Go to Leeds, and you'd find Bremner and Giles, or Manchester United, and immediately you think of Charlton, Stiles, Crerand, or down to Arsenal and pick up McLintock and Radford. They'd roll off your tongue.

Even at Everton years ago you had Vernon, Morrisey, Young, one or two others, they were all characters, players you could look up to. But now there doesn't seem to be that little bit of charisma knocking about.

When England won the World Cup in 1966 you had coaches crawling out of the walls, trying to teach kids how to kick a ball. Nobody ever taught me how to kick a ball, but they did teach me that there are certain ways of playing the game.

Now they get hold of youngsters at five or six and say, you've got to do it this way . . . and those kids grow up brainwashed. It's a fact that there are fewer personalities on the field who take it on themselves to do something off their own bat. Instead they wonder whether their coach or the manager will slang them and say, 'That's not your job.'

I was in the box against Middlesbrough when they had Mills, who was sold to West Brom for £500,000, playing for them; he had gone on a run down the wing, which to a Liverpool player would be a natural thing to do. Yet from the box they were calling him back, 'You haven't got to do that, we never taught you to do that.'

The lad was only trying to help someone but they didn't seem able to see it. Coaching has taken away an awful lot of initiative from players.

Liverpool players are taught to play within a system that doesn't tie them down. You could say to ninety per cent of Liverpool players, 'You play centre-forward today' and they'll have a go. And if you've got to chase fifty yards to stop somebody doing something and you're the one in a position to do it, you do it.

Allan Clarke was certainly one footballer I didn't really like on the field, because he was always the sly player, the schemer. We beat Leeds one day at Leeds, when they scored a goal and the ref disallowed it. It got shown later on 'Match of the Day'. I was going up for a ball with Clarkie when I noticed him getting ready to back-heel me. He'd done it to Larry Lloyd in a previous game at Anfield, so I read it right and stepped back. Both of us missed the ball and it was obvious to the ref what was going on. So even though somebody else put the ball in the net, he called it back and gave us a free kick.

But that was Clarkie all over. Even though he was a gifted player and good at scoring goals he would never do anything out in the open. He always reminded me of a sneak thief, the way he played.

There weren't many like him. You had fellows like Johnny Morrisey who played for Everton, of course, who would give and take. When we played Everton and Johnny was outside-left, you had to watch him. The rule was, if you're going to tackle him, do it properly. Don't go in at half-cock or he'll do you. At least you knew where you stood, or didn't, with Johnny.

11 England, My Disappointment

I suppose, looking back on it, I do regret not playing more games for England – I was in the squad enough times, on the bench. After so many Under-23 caps it would have been nice to gain more than just the one full international cap.

But Shanks always used to tell me, 'Concentrate on playing well for Liverpool and there'll always be a place for you here. Don't forget, it's Liverpool that pay your wages – not England.'

People ask me why I was passed over so many times – whether it was my tough image or whatever. I think basically there were just a lot of good wing-halfs knocking around at the time. I was maybe third or fourth in line behind Bobby Moore, Norman Hunter and Alan Mullery.

There's no disguising I was really disappointed not to get into the 1966 and 1970 World Cup squads – I was in the last forty but didn't make the final squad. And I knew then that basically no matter what I did I was never going to be an England regular.

But I hung on to what Shanks told me . . . 'England don't provide your bread and butter. You can always play for Liverpool, but you can't always play for England.' So gaining an England cap then changed from being an obsession with me to a point where I didn't give a damn.

I convinced myself that I'd won enough with Liverpool to make up for it. And quite frankly, these days, I think it's harder to win the European Cup, FA Cup or the League than it is to get an England cap.

They started giving England caps out to players who would never have made the Liverpool first team. There were an awful lot of good players knocking around ten years ago. I don't think there are that many good players knocking around now to warrant an automatic regular England place. And I think ten years ago an England cap was appreciated a damn sight more than it is now.

Some international players these days wouldn't have been considered at all in 1966, so drastically has the England scene changed – but I don't want to name names, or they'll be round our house with big sticks.

My one international cap came in 1971 against Wales in the home internationals – I was brought into the side along with a number of newly capped players, and my role basically was to stop big John Toshack. As it happens it was a no-score draw, a bad game.

Alf Ramsey was England manager then, and I believe in the Ramsey era. English football was magic. He got a formula together, he won the World Cup, and he did awfully well – a record like that is going to take some beating, no matter who's manager.

One year when I was captain of the Under-23s and Liverpool had a long season, Alf Ramsey came to Chris Lawler and I and said England were going on a tour and would we like to join the squad. We said 'No,' not through bad manners or anything, but because basically we were shattered and wanted a rest.

I suppose if the offer had come a couple of seasons before we would have found it hard to turn down, but by then Shanks had given us the confidence to turn round to someone like Ramsey and tell him truthfully how we felt.

That still didn't stop Ramsey calling us a 'couple of prize prigs'! I'm afraid all we did then was go round the corner after he'd gone and have a good laugh. But I expect it was partly his frustration at not being able to take the players he wanted.

Some people say that incident had a bearing on my future international career – I don't think it did. Chris went on to get a dozen England caps and I had a rewarding time with the Under-23s.

To a certain extent, of course, I regret not playing for England more, but I think I would regret it more if Liverpool had not done so well. Winning so many honours with Liverpool made up for a lack of England caps for me. I suppose I'm a successful club player who played once for England, rather than a successful international who's won nothing.

There are players in the England squad now who've never won a medal and probably never will. I think one England cap from the era when I played is worth a lot more than it is today.

It's a funny game – you take Ian Callaghan, who got a couple of England caps around the time I did. He had to wait until he was in his mid-thirties before he got any more. Absolutely crazy!

But getting back to Alf Ramsey – he was probably one of the best managers I've known. I was shocked when he got the push. He gave England the respect they wanted and deserved, and had the courage and foresight not to desert them when they weren't doing so well. I respect Ramsey – I think he's a hell of a fellow. He knew what he was doing and he had the guts to get on with it. And he certainly would not have deserted a sinking ship the way Revie did.

Revie was a good manager at Leeds but with England it was a different kettle of fish – he had players from different clubs coming together and he found he couldn't mould them in the same way he could a club side. It was hard for him, but whether he was going to be a success or not didn't make up for him saying, 'I'm off.' No matter what he says now, he'll never be held in the same esteem again. What upset so many people was not so much his going as the way he went.

I don't think he did England any favours – international football took a turn for the worse in fact. Mind you, he was always a decent fellow whenever I met him, but somewhere along the line the pound notes seem to have taken over his brain.

I actually played against him once. One of his last games was for Leeds reserves at Anfield when I was a youngster in

Liverpool's reserve side. We beat them about 8–0 . . . perhaps that's what made him give up playing!

In reaching the finals of the European Championship, Ron Greenwood became the most successful England manager since Ramsey, but his real test will still come with the next World Cup.

He has repaired a lot of the damage to our football reputation, which Revie left in tatters, but he's still not safe in the job by any means. England still doesn't instill the sort of confidence that makes you think you can go out there and batter the opposition, the confidence they showed the year they won the 1966 World Cup.

Greenwood has to rely on certain key players to knit the side together and in that he's lucky to have world-class players like Keegan, Clemence and Shilton.

Kevin Keegan stands out more than anybody, for no one else seems to stamp the same authority on what they're doing on the pitch than he does. If anybody is needed to speak for England at the moment the press usually go to Keegan, or they talk about Clem and Shilton. I only hope the three of them stick around and are still at their peak for the next World Cup. Nobody sticks in my brain as being on the same par with them in this country.

Greenwood is basically a nice fellow who did quite well at West Ham and created a good footballing side, bringing on some good players like Bobby Moore, Geoff Hurst and Martin Peters. He's still doing quite well, but his sides never seem to have that confident, competitive edge and I would say he's still not that secure . . . but then what manager is?

Of the other home international sides, Scotland probably have more hard men than any, though a lot of skill also comes out of Scotland. What they suffer from as an international side is an inability to play together because they're stubborn, and the team suffers because they all play like individuals.

Yet if someone has a go at one of their team they have this ability to fight together, like a pack of wolves. If someone turns on one of them, the whole lot go on the prowl. But if nobody disturbs them they each play their own game, and that's probably where they suffer.

In the last World Cup they suffered from big headaches more than anything. They got a bit cocky, strutting round saying, 'England haven't got here, Wales haven't got here, Northern Ireland haven't got here . . . ' and then they got beaten by the likes of . . . well, they should have been pulling together again, instead of relaxing at the wrong time. It's a shame, because Scotland in the past four or five years has developed a better team than England, a stronger team, but they need that bit of needle. They say there's nothing worse than an angry Scot.

England never quite recovered from winning the World Cup in 1966. They went to Mexico in 1970 but since then it's been downhill all the way. In England we suffer from over-caution and they still lack a winning system. They tried to play like Liverpool play, but the only way to do that is field eleven Liverpool players, because any others are inept at copying such a strong team. Liverpool wouldn't have been champions for so many years, if others could play like they can.

12 Managers and Directors

To be a successful manager you really have to be a bit of a bastard. As Archie Gemmell said about Brian Clough, 'Some days I really hate the fellow, but I'd die for him all the same . . .' as I would have done for Shanks or Paisley. It's as simple as that.

Brian Clough, I would say, is quite willing to shock people into making them believe he is hard and ruthless, when in fact he's only a stickler for discipline. I remember hearing Clough at a dinner in Swansea shortly after his publicized row with Larry Lloyd – someone asked him if it was childish to insist Larry wore a Notts Forest club blazer. And Brian said, 'I'm manager of a club that's done nothing for years. All I'm trying to do is get some discipline in. I pay him good money and in return one of the things I'd like him to do is wear a club blazer. I'm not asking him to go to bed in it, or go dancing in it, or go to the pictures in it. I don't even want to argue with him about it. I don't want to fight him. All I want him to do is put on a blazer and represent Nottingham Forest.'

But if you imagine Nottingham Forest walking down the road in their smart blazers and Liverpool walking with them in casual clothes, most folk are going to say, 'Who's that team walking along the road with Liverpool?'

Also if such an incident over that blazer had happened at Anfield, a quick word in the player's ear would have been enough – 'Don't do it again, son, okay?' – and it would never have reached the newspapers.

But that's Brian Clough all over – he's trying to get recognition for his players, and in return he's insisting they appear neat and tidy. To a certain extent he's imitating Shankly – he has the same dream of building a team for stardom as Shankly did – but Shanks never had to insist on tidiness. He put his players on a pedestal, made them feel good, and tidiness came naturally.

Brian Clough's methods work to a certain extent, but sometimes he gets lost in his own importance and I'd say that's what spoils him. He's lowered the blinds on lots of aspects of the modern game, and given outsiders an insight into things they might not appreciate. But he's a personality in a game that's woefully short of characters these days – I admire the fellow for certain things he's done. But he also had to learn the hard way, and sometimes his own impetuosity gets the better of him.

When he went to Leeds I don't think he realized he was going to a place where the players were running the club – and that was his only big mistake. Revie had created a team where you could rely on the players, as you can rely on the Liverpool players today.

It wasn't a case of keeping an eye on them all the time, telling them what to do. Clough, in his frustration, seemed to want to discipline them, but the likes of Charlton, Bremner, Madeley, Cooper and Hunter didn't need disciplining. So what developed was a conflict between the boss and the players. I believe Clough could have had the England job by now if he'd been a bit more diplomatic. He kept his mouth shut for twelve months. If he'd kept it shut another twelve he might have been preferred to Ron Greenwood.

He packed in the Under-23s job because he didn't have the time to give to it – well that's what he says, but there's one thing Cloughie's not, and that's stupid.

He perhaps read between the lines and thought, 'Well, if I can't have the top job, then sod it.' You think about it, if Ron Greenwood doesn't succeed in a few years they're going to be looking for a replacement anyway, and if you're a successful manager of a successful First Division club you probably stand a better chance than if you've been associated with Greenwood in a minor capacity.

So everything Clough does you've got to think twice about, weigh it up . . .

I suppose in lots of ways I've been lucky with managers. I've only really had two in my playing career – Bill Shankly and Bob Paisley. There's been John Toshack at Swansea, of course, and he was the main reason I went to Swansea, because I knew him as a player and a colleague. But although I respect him for what he's doing at Swansea I still don't regard him as a manager in the same way as I think of Shanks and Bob.

Shanks was one of the greatest characters of the game. You could be in a room filled with lords and ladies and Shanks would walk in, looking for all the world like Jimmy Cagney in his new mac – and people would stop what they were saying and look his way.

Bill Shankly probably took more on himself than a lot of other managers. As I've said, he had a hand not only in organizing the teams but also the training facilities, the staff, a whole lot of things. When things were at their peak, because he liked to have his finger on everything I don't think even he realized the pressure the job was exerting on him.

He spent Liverpool FC's money wisely, too. We never had a gymnasium – Shanks never believed in training indoors because you don't play football indoors. You play football on a wet pitch, a boggy pitch, a rock-hard icy pitch – 'You're going to play on it Saturday, you'll train on it today' was his attitude.

They say Shanks was a legend in his own lifetime – that's true, and the confidence he oozed was unbelieveable. He believed totally in Liverpool FC and was always proud of Anfield, even to the extent of putting a sign up over the tunnel to the pitch saying 'This is Anfield'.

People would come to the ground and he'd show them round and they'd come to the toilets and he would flush the bowl, look at his watch and tell them, 'And it takes exactly thirty seconds to fill up again.' It was just his way – he knew every detail about that ground.

Mind you, the pressures on Bob Paisley when he took over from Shanks were enormous – the pressures to win something. I don't think even the players realized at first how vital it was that we win something for Bob to get the ghost of Shanks off his back.

And you have to give Bob credit for respecting what Shanks had created. He let everybody carry on doing their own thing, and gradually introduced new players, new methods.

There was never any confrontation at Anfield, like there was at Manchester City between Joe Mercer and Malcolm Allison. When Joe left, the club went right down and didn't win anything because Allison wasn't content to build on what was there – he threw out the good with the bad and it hasn't worked.

But Bob was content to do things quietly – if we hadn't won trophies under Bob it might have been a different story, but we avoided the troubles City had, and that came about to a large extent through Bob's attitude. Everything we've won in recent years you can put down to Paisley's common sense, but the roots are still Shankly's. Bob Paisley has done well to maintain Liverpool's record since Shanks left. He's made one or two good buys, but he never started out with a clean sweep – he knew who was good for the club. After all, he helped build the club with Bill Shankly.

Bob Paisley is a bit quieter than Shanks and doesn't shout so much when Liverpool FC get beaten, but he still gets annoyed. Mind you, Shanks probably said enough during his fifteen years as manager for Bob not to bother – he just gets on with the job.

And although there's been a lot of fuss made of Liverpool FC, when I was there a certain humble atmosphere still seemed to predominate, like it all hadn't gone to the lads' heads. There were never any tantrums or squabbles, no fuss. Liverpool never gave you the impression they'd get into the sort of position Manchester City found themselves in, where they had to go out and spend £1½ million on a new team.

Bob Paisley gets just as nervous before a game as Shanks used to. He says things he doesn't really mean, and rambles on a bit, coming out with some quaint sayings of his own, and all because he's a little bit nervous, that's all.

One day we were playing Barcelona in Spain and we were having a team meeting and chatting about their squad; going through their side, Bob comes to this player and says, 'Now this fellow – he's not very fast, but he's nippy!'

Well, with him being the boss, you don't like to upset him, you know, but now and again you have to laugh, and it helps relieve the tension too. Like we were playing a vital League game and we were all together in Liverpool's Holiday Inn, and everyone was speculating what the team was going to be when the boss comes in and says, 'Well lads, I don't honestly know who's playing till I get to the ground.' And everyone can see his nerves are twitching a bit and he suddenly realizes he's got the *Liverpool Echo* sticking out of his pocket. There'd been a bit of speculation, naturally, in the press about the team, so he suddenly takes it out, throws it on the table and says, 'Tell you what, I'll go and ring the *Echo* up and see what the side is . . . see who they want us to play!' It was funny at the time and helped ease the pressure for us as well as him.

Although I played under only two managers at Liverpool I have, of course, met other managers when they've come to Anfield or we've gone to their grounds, and over the years you get to know them pretty well.

Lawrie McMenemy, who gets on with his job, won promotion for Southampton, won the FA Cup and got to the League Cup final, doesn't make a fuss – people make a fuss of him – and he speaks a lot of sense. I think he sounds not bad at all.

I've met Jock Stein many a time, up in Scotland and down here. He was at Leeds for a while, and before that created the marvellous Celtic side, moulded them into a fighting force that won the European Cup. So I think Jock Stein has got something.

But then you take the likes of John Bond at Norwich. He's had a good go at doing things, but still won nothing, and every time a professional team goes to play them he slangs the opposition. I think it's fear – he tries to convince his players the opposition are rubbish, even after they've beaten his team.

Harry Catterick, at Everton, always gave me the impression

he was a lounge-suit manager, but every time you saw him on the telly he'd have a track-suit on. The Everton lads used to say he kept his track-suit hanging up behind his office door for the television! If they ever interviewed Shanks before a Derby game, he'd always come up sweating from a five-a-side, but Harry always appeared unruffled, cool, calm and collected.

I didn't like the look of Billy Bingham. I don't know what it was, but the job seemed too dirty for him somehow. He never gave the impression he would put his track-suit on and do his little bit – but he was always quite nice when he spoke.

Now Gordon Lee, he's a sincere fellow, and he always tries to give confidence. But he probably lacks that bit of charisma, and he doesn't always come over with that confidence you expect in a manager of a big club like Everton. Nor does he seem to enjoy it much either. He gets his track-suit on and he gets stuck in, but he's always got the expression on his face that football is such a serious business you daren't laugh. Every time we played Everton, when he was manager, I always thought they were terrified of Liverpool, because Lee is a great Liverpool fan. And they always seemed terrified of being beaten, for fear he'd take them in after the game and lock them in a darkened room for punishment. They got so uptight in the end that you'd win quite easily.

It's not always that easy to make the transition from player to manager. Take Jackie Charlton, for instance – when he took over at Middlesbrough he inherited a team that were destined for First Division football anyway. Then when they got there he fell into the trap that a lot of managers fall into – he wanted to consolidate their success so he surrounded himself with defensive players, and once he'd got himself trapped, he couldn't get out. Instead of having a team that could do a bit, he ended up with a team that was just surviving in the division, and playing with eleven defenders.

His brother Bobby maybe went the other way, and never got to grips with management because he finished playing too soon. He's still a very fit person, but to me he'll always be a worrier – as a manager he seemed to develop lines in his head, always had a frown on. I've got to know Bobby pretty well since he stopped playing, and I think he suffered from what I don't want to suffer from. It's very hard to be both a manager and a player. I don't think he was ever cut out to be a manager anyway and since he left the management side he's become something like his old self.

I've had offers to manage a couple of teams, but I suppose at the back of my mind I've always thought that I enjoy playing too much and I'm not that interested in a seven-day-a-week job.

Footballers don't have to do much except keep themselves fit, but the manager probably has to go into the office at nine, sorting out the mail, phone calls, team selections, training. If you've got a good staff they can ease some of the problems, but people want you to do all sorts of different things, whether you're the biggest or the smallest club in the land – opening fêtes and that. Players get asked and managers seem to get asked a damn sight more. If players get asked they have to ask the boss if they can go, so he has this extra problem of deciding who can go and who can't. And you've got new lads coming through and people injured and you've got to decide what to do with them. Then you might do a spot of training, have a bite of lunch, then a meeting with the directors, arranging travelling with the secretary . . . and that's only Monday to Friday.

You've got the game on Saturday, and all the worry of whether we'll win, lose or draw. Then on Sunday you come in to see who's injured and start planning for the next match. So it's a never-ending job and takes a special kind of person to be able to do it.

I never really wanted to play for any team other than Liverpool. I knew Brian Clough was after me when he was at Derby, because he told me one year, and I knew Birmingham were after me because I'd spoken to Willie Bell, and I knew Arsenal were after me, and Manchester United got a mention in the newspapers.

But I never wanted to leave Liverpool – they are the best side, no question about that, and I don't think Shanks had any intention of letting me go anyway.

If Shanks taught me a lot, there was somebody at Liverpool

who taught me more, and that was Joe Fagan.

Joe Fagan is probably the top coach in Europe, even the world. To me he was like a silent partner in business, authoritative, knowing when to say something, knowing when to keep his mouth shut . . . he's been at Liverpool twenty-odd years now and if there's anybody who's done more work for the club I'd like to meet him.

I respected Joe above everyone else, probably because he had an attitude towards football that was all Liverpool. And if there was anything to be done, whereas others might do it in a week, Joe seemed able to do it in an hour. Joe's one of those backroom lads who hardly ever get a mention, yet he probably knows more about football than anybody I've ever met. I've had reason to be grateful to him on more than one occasion for cooling me down or making me see sense.

When he was in charge of the reserves and I needed a clip over the ear, I'd get one, and at the same time when I needed a bit of praise, or a bit of tutoring, a bit of coaching, that was there too.

Ronnie Moran goes about things a different way to Joe, but he still gets results. Roy Evans to a certain extent is the same. When he first started he was a bit shy, but now he's got that quality where you can be friendly with the lads, but also know when to show a bit of iron fist. It's all right laughing and joking with the lads, but somewhere along the line the laughing's got to stop and you've got to get down to the serious business of being successful.

If you want success, you're talking about Bob Paisley for England manager, but thankfully I don't think Bob is that interested in the England job. He and the rest of his staff have been associated with Liverpool for a long time, and they're ambitious for Liverpool more than anything else.

You look at Liverpool's record twenty years ago and you could fit it on the back of a postage stamp. You look at it now and you can write a book about it.

As for directors, I was only about seventeen when I decided I didn't particularly like them. Liverpool were entered in the Lancashire Senior Cup competition, and the club weren't really keen on us getting that far, because there were other things they wanted us to concentrate on, so the A team played in most of the ties.

We still ended up getting to the final and we played Burnley at Turf Moor. Tommy Lawrence had broken his fingers so Hamish McKenzie went in goal and saved a penalty. In the end it was a tight game – remember we were only teenagers playing Burnley's full reserve side – and we were beaten 2–1.

So Bob Lord, who is Burnley's chairman, had to present the trophy to his own side, and the way he was hugging it you'd have thought it was the FA Cup. Probably he thought it was some compensation for them having lost the FA Cup that year – but there was no word of sympathy for the losers. Ours was the bigger achievement that day, even though we lost, but we just didn't exist so far as he was concerned.

I've always said directors should be there to direct and not pick teams. Any director who tries to meddle in the playing or managerial side of the club doesn't deserve his place on the board. I've found in my career with Liverpool FC that everyone from the directors to the groundstaff, know what their own job is, and do it well. It's an attitude that has contributed to the club's success.

I used to think most of them didn't care tuppence about football, and certainly some of them never knew the players. I remember one director stopping Alan A'Court getting on the team coach when Alan was a lad and starting out to play for Liverpool. 'Come on now, off you get,' said this director. 'No autograph hunters allowed, sonny . . . '

Another time we were in New York with the team, rounding the corner by the hotel where we were staying, and another director stopped Ian Callaghan and me in the street, looks at Ian and says, 'Hello, Frankie. Didn't know you were still with us. How are you?' He'd mistaken Cally for Frankie Twiss, who used to play for Liverpool some while back – I suppose they did look a little alike.

But as time has gone on, the Liverpool directors, as I said, have learnt to live with success and got the business machine at Anfield rolling smoothly, to everyone's benefit. And I would put the directors at Swansea on an equal par with the directors at Anfield – they, too, have the right approach to the job.

But no director is still that unapproachable that he can't be brought down to earth now and again. Bill Shankly, who is no respector of persons anyway, was really annoyed with one director's vociferous criticisms during a game at Anfield, directed at a certain Liverpool player who was having a really bad off-day.

His comments needled Shanks, who stormed into the board-room after the game and ranted, 'Did you hear that stupid so-and-so. . . ?' When somebody points out the fellow he's slating is standing behind him, Shanks wheels round, looks him in the eye and says, 'Aye, that's the bugger!'

13 Euro-Hero

Liverpool FC is rightly proud of its European record. We've been in European competitions longer and more consistently than any other English club and came so close to winning a unique treble – the League Championship, the FA Cup and the European Cup all in one season – that I doubt if it will ever be achieved now by any other club.

I was lucky, too, in that Liverpool's first European Cup run coincided with my getting a regular first-team place. At the beginning of the 1964 season Shanks was still trying to get the formula right, mould us into a prize-winning squad. I was tried in a couple of different positions and played in a few league games – I was happy to, for I reasoned if I couldn't get in while the lads were playing average I had no chance if they hit a winning streak without me.

I was getting my game sorted out. The main thing in football is not to lose your concentration. You have to think constantly about the game – what will happen if so-and-so mis-kicks this ball? What will happen if I move out of position now? What will happen if so-and-so receives this pass?

A lot of players have brilliant ball-control but they can't play because they lack this ability to think ahead. Give them the ball and they look brilliant, magic. Without the ball they look lost – some of them might as well be corner flags.

So I thought I might just be on to a winner here. All I had to do was keep my concentration, get stuck in, get involved, and hope for the breaks.

As it happened, Liverpool began their European Cup run against the Iceland team, Reykjavik, beat them quite easily and then drew the Belgium side Anderlecht in the second round. Now Shanks had been to see them and knew they were a good side – quite a few of their team were Belgium internationals.

And it was Ronnie Moran who first said to me, 'You're playing when we meet Anderlecht. The boss wants you to be Ronnie Yeats's right leg.' Sure enough we had a meeting and Shanks told me, 'You're right-half, don't move out of there,' and I ended up with no. 10 on my back.

Liverpool were the first to use the 4–4–2 system, which I think confused people for a long time, especially the continental sides. I was inside-left with no. 10 on, but dropping back to right-half. It was done because Shanks didn't believe in swapping jerseys round for the sake of it.

But I can still remember Anderlecht had a lad called Paul Van Himst, and another called Jurier, who used to play in glasses, taping them on. Van Himst, who had more caps for Belgium than anyone else, came up to me during the game, pointed at his head and then at me and said, 'You . . . crazy. . . .'

They couldn't really understand our tactics, and we beat them by confusing them. I was enthralled by the game, determined not to lose my concentration, taking in how the continental lads liked to play and countering their moves by anticipation. I found in the end I was tackling this lad Van Himst harder whenever he came near me.

After the game the boss said I was learning fast, and that I hadn't done badly, which pleased me no end . . . then he left me out of the next league game against Spurs!

The following week, however, I remember going on the coach to Burnley for a league game, and it was always the twelfth man's job to carry the skips with the kit in off the coach. Bob Paisley saw me lifting them and said, 'You want to save your strength.' I didn't carry the skips very often after that. In fact that was really the start of my regular first-team career.

We continued our European Cup run against Cologne, and then in the first leg of the semi-finals we met Inter-Milan at Anfield.

Chris Lawler was playing right-back that season and I eventually ended up at right-half – it was the first full season for both of us. Then Chris got married the day before we were due to play Inter-Milan and ended up spending his wedding night rooming with me! It must have worked because we beat the Italians 3–1. It all seemed so easy.

Then we had to travel to San Siro Stadium in Milan for the second leg . . . and we were cheated rotten that night by some really cruel refereeing. People often ask me what was my biggest disappointment in football, and I always single out that semi-final return match because of the way we were robbed.

It started, in fact, the minute we got to Milan. The papers were full of stories about Liverpool FC being on drugs, making us out to be real animals. We stayed out of town, but the fans found our hotel and kept us awake with hooters, rattles and waving placards in the middle of the night. We frankly found it frightening, and it took us all of ten years to get used to all their tricks – the chants and the hooters, no paper in the toilets at the ground, that sort of thing. . . .

At San Siro Stadium (which incidentally was the pre-determined venue for the final) we knew as soon as we arrived there was just no way Inter-Milan were going to lose. The crowd were throwing fireworks, bottles, anything they could lay their hands on.

There was a Spanish referee, and we thought we'd made a good start, until Tommy Lawrence gathered the ball, one of the Milan players flicked it away from him and put it in the net. The ref decided that was a goal. Years later when I was on the bench for an England *v.* Ireland game, Georgie Best did exactly the same thing to Gordon Banks and it was disallowed – as it should be.

The second goal was scored direct from an indirect free-kick, and given. Then we scored a goal, a good goal, and he disallowed it. It was obvious whose side he was on. I still remember grabbing the referee after our goal – I was sorely tempted to punch him – but he never booked anybody. He wasn't interested.

Milan went on to score the third goal they needed and we were so disappointed it was untrue. As we were walking down the tunnel someone threw a bottle out of the crowd – it missed me but, more important, it missed the ref as well. Like I said, nothing went right . . .

What upset us more was that there was never anything done about it. The press were full of it – Liverpool were blatantly robbed of a European Cup final place. Inter-Milan went on to beat Benfica in the final at San Siro, but they'd still committed this crime in front of so many thousand people, and got away with it. It was sickening.

We'd won the FA Cup that year so we were in Europe again in the Cup Winners' Cup and we got to the final of that which made up for Milan to a certain extent. The final was at Hampden Park and we were beaten 2–1 by Borussia Dortmund – we didn't play well, and it wasn't a good game. When you lose it's never a good game anyway!

We had our share of European shocks. In the 1966–7 European Cup competition we played Ajax on their ground – and it was hellishly foggy. You couldn't see from goal-mouth to goal-mouth at times. In fact Shanks ran on to the field at one point to talk to Ron Yeats and ran off again without the referee spotting him. We were battered 5–1, but it wasn't really a freak result. We could manage only a draw with them in the return leg at Anfield. We just happened to catch Ajax at the time when they were starting to be good.

Perhaps we were a little over-confident because we'd done so well in the European Cup Winners' Cup the previous season by reaching the final. In fact, half-way through the 1965–6 season there was talk of us doing the treble – we were in Europe, we were handily placed in the League – but then Chelsea went and knocked us out in the third round of the FA Cup. So that was an end to it.

I have a particular memory of the 1970 Fairs Cup-tie against Ferencvaros – we drew 1–1 at home and finished off no-score away from home. Conditions were terrible – bumpy ground, we were playing badly, they were playing badly. It was an awful game. There was a concrete trench round the ground, and the kids stood on boxes looking over the edge; whenever the ball went off the park these kids would dive down into the trench and fetch it back. At one point the ball went out of play and a kid went to get it for me. Someone from the crowd yelled out to the kid, encouraging him to lob it further along the trench, so I had a go at him: 'You stupid little sod. Give us the ball back.' Then I felt a tap on my shoulder.

I thought somebody wanted a word with me so I turned round – but there was nobody there. About a yard away, however, I spied a brandy bottle on the ground. Everything went through my mind at once . . . I remembered Moenchengladbach playing an Italian team when the same thing happened; they played the match again and the other team won . . . so I thought, we'll get another game out of this, and threw a wobbler.

I wasn't injured or anything but I threw a dive. The referee and the linesman came over, and they just didn't want to know. They're not going back to Hungary whatever happens, so they flicked the bottle away.

And the fellow in the crowd who threw it? Well, he suddenly got the plague. The crowd just parted and pointed, 'It's him, not me, it's him.' The police went in and hauled him out and started laying into him.

A couple of minutes later they blew for full time and I was going off when I saw their big inside-left. This fellow had been kicking me all the game and I really had a cob on by then, so I said to Ronnie Moran, 'I'm gonna belt him. I've had enough of him. I'm gonna go for him.'

Just then another fellow ran out of the crowd, from behind the goal where the dressing-rooms were, and the police dived in and started knocking hell out of him. I thought, 'Forget it. That's it. I don't want to know.'

There was a FIFA inquiry and I ended up with a two-match ban. The lad who lobbed the bottle at me got six month's gaol, plus a good beating-up . . . it was a shame, because the bottle was probably the only shot that was on target all afternoon!

I remember also when we beat Borussia to win the UEFA Cup in 1972–3 – it was chaos! At the end of the match they pushed a table on to the pitch and presented me, as captain of Liverpool, with the trophy, a huge, heavy thing and difficult to lift, let alone carry. They handed out the medals with a minimum of ceremony because by then half the spectators were over the wire and all around us. I then trotted off on a victory lap trying to hold this cup, with fans hanging on to my shirt and hair. I've never been so glad to get back to the dressing-room.

One secret I managed to keep fairly well over the years stemmed back to the time when I was thirteen or fourteen and playing for Liverpool Juniors in a friendly against Manchester Schoolboys at Stockton Heath. I got butted in the face by their big centre-forward, who loosened my teeth.

They were still quite healthy but in those days, if your teeth were damaged, they came out, no messing. It wasn't a case of trying to save them. In taking them out they dragged out part of my gum. So I ended up with a couple of false teeth. They probably helped me on the pitch – because after that you'd never get a smile out of me, as I was too conscious of these missing teeth!

It became a regular thing between me and Ronnie Moran at the big games that I would wrap my teeth in a bit of bandage and give them to him to keep till after the match. If we were going out at Wembley for Cup finals, for instance, I'd take a piece of bandage stuffed into my shorts, wait till the presentations were over, take my teeth out and wrap them up for Ronnie. He was always the first person I'd look for when the final whistle blew.

After that glorious European Cup final in Rome, I've got a memorable photograph of me being hoisted in the air at the end of the game by Ronnie; it looks like we're celebrating, but what I'm really saying to him is, 'Put me down, you soft bugger! Where's me bloody teeth?' Luckily, the way the flash has gone off you can't tell whether I've got any teeth in at all!

If I didn't smile a lot, you certainly couldn't say the same about Shanks. No matter where we were playing, in European competition or a friendly, if things got rough, you could always rely on Shanks to give you a smile or two. He always felt he could do anything – he was always full of confidence, and even when he couldn't speak the language abroad he could make himself understood.

We were playing the last game of a pre-season tour in Germany, against Hanover or somewhere, and this team got stuck into us, so I got stuck into them. At half-time the ref thinks he's had enough of this, so he comes across to Shanks and says, 'Smith – no. 4 – one bad tackle more – off!'

Shanks looks him in the eye and in the same broken English, with lots of arm waving, tells him, 'Smith – if he off – everybody off!' We had no bother after that and eventually won 4–1.

We played one time in Romania and it was very warm. Shanks asked the waiters to give the lads Coke, only to be told there were just a couple of bottles left. All they had was Vichy water, which is too gassy for me, and none of the others were keen on it.

So Shanks goes on the prowl, and in the kitchen he finds crates of Coke. Grabbing one of the waiters, he says, 'You give these to my lads or I'll . . . or I'll report you to the Kremlin!'

Another time we were playing in Vancouver in the Olympic Stadium against the German team Eintracht and all hell was let loose – Shanks had been told the Germans liked to play with a soft ball, and their goalkeeper carried a little deflator around with him. Chances were if you saw him handling the ball, he was letting it down.

Well, we tossed up and were changing ends when their goalkeeper, who was about 6 ft 3 ins, ran past me and picked the ball up. Shanks was on his feet in a flash and running across to him from the touchline. In his broad Scottish he started laying into him: 'You scheming bugger! Put that ball down or I'll kick you right where it hurts!'

He held out his hands for the ball and the German gave it to him straight away, but he had nothing else in his hands and truthfully didn't know what all the fuss was about. Shanks must have realized that he'd made a mistake, because he trotted off to the centre-spot, put the ball down and ran back to his seat.

We drew 1–1, it was a bad game. Reuben Bennett was with us

on the bench, and he was always a bit of a hard man, a bit of a boxer in his day. Ian St John got sent off and the German trainer decided to have a go at Reuben, swinging a couple of punches which Reuben ducked – brilliant. We all said afterwards it was a good job Reuben had had the sense not to hit him back or he'd have flattened him and then we really would have been in trouble.

But there's nothing like a pre-match briefing to lighten the mood if you are feeling down. I remember the year we played Moenchengladbach in a European semi-final leg at Anfield and Bob Paisley was going through the team. At the time I was thirty-three and Cally was about thirty-five and the boss was saying . . . 'this Bertie Vogts, he's no good, he's over the hill, he's thirty-two now. And this other fellow, Klinghammer, he must be thirty-five . . . then there's Bonhoff. He's on the way out. He's all of twenty-nine. . . .'

Cally and I were sinking lower in our seats, when Joe Fagan turned round and burst out laughing. He said, 'Cheer up! You're as old as you feel.' I said, 'Right now I feel like I'm sixty-four!'

14 Rowdies, Wowdies and Fannies

I first went to America just before I got married. I was only a lad of eighteen, and I went on tour with Liverpool because Roger Hunt, Gordon Milne and Peter Thompson were away with the international squad.

It turned out to be quite a violent introduction to the States. We played about ten games in five weeks – I played in seven of them, and it was around the time I was challenging for a regular first-team place. We stayed in New York for a time, sharing rooms. Ian St John and Ron Yeats had cameras and a few other things stolen, so we were very wary after that.

Then in Chicago it happened again. Tommy Lawrence shared a room with Alf Arrowsmith; they'd been out one night and had a few drinks, and when they came in Tommy packed his clothes away like he always did and was first in bed, while Alfie just threw his trousers over a chair before going to sleep.

Come the morning Tommy woke first and went to put Alfie's trousers on – then realized it wasn't his pair, as it also dawned on him that they were the only pair in the room, virtually the only clothes in the room.

They'd been burgled during the night and were cleaned out, in common with one or two of the other lads. Funnily enough, Alan A'Court had been going to his room late that night and seen a fellow walking down the back stairs carrying all sorts of suitcases, but just hadn't put two and two together. They lost their passports and everything.

After a trip to Boston we came back to New York again. In the afternoon I told Chris Lawler I was going up to lie down for a bit, because the humidity was a bit much. I was feeling flaked out.

Next thing is I hear this key in the door, and I immediately think – burglars again. So I'm looking round for something to belt him with. I took my shoe off and stood on the dressing-table behind the door as it slowly opened – scared to death.

And as the door opened slowly, Chris sneaked in. He was a bit apprehensive because he knew I'd come up to lie down, but he couldn't see me and wondered what the hell was going on. He was very lucky I didn't belt him over the head, but that experience made us all very jumpy, because we were only lads.

But America did have its better moments. Like when we stayed in Chicago in this big hotel built round four sides of a courtyard. Chris and I were looking out of our window one night quite late when most people still had their windows open or hadn't pulled their blinds – and we saw this fellow hanging out of one window, with a pair of binoculars. We realized he must be a peeping Tom, and when we looked around there were one or two more blimping other rooms, having a good look.

So we looked at each other, eased our window up slow and I said, 'Right, shout and see what happens . . . one, two . . . *Aargh! You dirty buggers!*

And three or four people all at once shot back in, slammed their windows and yanked the blinds across. Lights were going on everywhere. It was just like one of those mad movies.

During our tour, we travelled from New York to Boston, St Louis, Chicago and Detroit – where Chris and I got picked up for jaywalking. We just didn't know we were doing wrong – we walked across the road on the lights and the policeman picked us up and about four others at the same time. He fined the others on the spot, but took us back to the hotel, gave us a dressing-down, and let us off.

The first things Shanks wanted to see in America were Jack Dempsey's bar, Al Capone's car and Boot Hill . . . probably not realizing that every town in cowboy territory has its own Boot Hill.

One time Bill Shankly was coming into New York some two weeks after the rest of us, and he refused to fix his watch, insisting, 'I'm Bill Shankly. I'm King of the May like' and that the difference in hours has nothing to do with him. He was going to bed at what he thought was ten o'clock – in fact nearer four in the afternoon – having his eight hours and getting up at what he thought was six in the morning – it was midnight. He couldn't understand why everybody was off to bed when he was just getting up. 'Where are you all going?' he would say. But he became used to it after a while.

America didn't immediately impress me – it had its good and bad points. When we were in New York it was World Fair year, and it was positively the worst spectacle I've ever been to. I went with Phil Chisnell and Phil Fearns – two lads we called Budweiss and Shaeffer, because they liked to drink American beer – and all we seemed to do was prop up the bar during the time we spent at the Fair.

After that I thought, I've seen America, I've had it. I went home and got married.

Much later I went back to America again. Brian Hall and I went out to do football clinics in Milwaukee, taking our wives and kids, and enjoyed ourselves. We must have impressed the Americans that time, so much so that we got offers to go out there and play.

A lad called Beau Rogers, who is general manager of Tampa Bay Rowdies in Florida, came across to Liverpool to sign me up one summer, and we had a spot of lunch together with another lad from the press.

Now often American words don't mean the same as ours, and we were sat there and Beau was explaining the set-up at Tampa. 'We've got the team, and they're called the Rowdies,' he said, 'And then we've got our cheer-leaders, the dancing-girls, and we call them the Wowdies, and then we've got our fans, and we call them our Fannies . . .' And we just fell about laughing.

But I enjoyed Beau's company and being in America when I

went over there to play. Whereas the big things, the overall plan, may be organized, sometimes they fall down on details. When I flew out to Florida first of all, it was Bicentennial holiday time and most folk were away. There to meet us was one of the secretaries from Beau's office, and she had a photograph so she could pick me out. When I stepped off the aeroplane and this girl came up and said, 'You're Tommy Smith,' I thought, 'This can't be bad. I've only just arrived and I get recognized already.'

She had a car there to take me and the family to our flat, but when we got the bags in the boot, she turned and said, 'Look, I feel a bit embarrassed about this. It's been a bit of a rush getting here, and the office is closed and I haven't had time to go to the bank. Can you lend me some money to get some petrol?' So I thought, 'This is a good start . . . '

But we soon settled in, terrific. The children really loved it in Florida, but Susie wasn't so keen on the bugs. Florida is in the tropics, and everything's big – big oranges, big melons, big flies, big grasshoppers . . . their bluebottles are about four times as big as ours and the grasshoppers look like they could hop half-a-mile. You had to put bath plugs in before you went to bed so the bugs wouldn't get up the drains, buy all these sprays, and be careful what food you left out. But it was a good place to live, plenty going on, plenty to do, lovely beaches. I enjoyed it.

I also met Rodney Marsh again. He was out there playing for the Rowdies too – a real character, the crowd loved him. He loves his football but he's always been a little bit crazy in his outlook, always that little bit mixed up. You could never really get on his wavelength, never talk his language, which always seemed to be half-way between Freud and Donald Duck. He'd be talking about one thing, change in midstream, talk about something else, then go back . . . I think the only person who sometimes understood Rodney was Rodney himself. He would do things purely and solely to surprise you. We'd go on a trip to New York for a couple of days, and he would bring along a big bag that could hold a suit and all that business – and inside he'd have nothing except a toothbrush and a tube of toothpaste. And he never wore socks.

But he was a likeable fellow and had a fine sense of humour. He used to tell us the story of when Tony Book had just taken over at Manchester City, and he always seemed to go around with a frown on his face. So Rodney got one of those tee-shirts printed 'Give us a smile, Bookie'.

Tony must have thought about it, gone home that night and got some sticky cut-out letters and stuck them over his own tee-shirt. Marshie said when Tony came in the next morning it was hilarious because half the letters were hanging off. And it read 'You play and I'll smile'.

One thing that did bug me about Tampa, though, was their goalkeeper, Arnie Mausser. Now Big Arnie was always the type who was going to let the odd goal in, and he was never keen to come off his line. For instance, if we won it would be 2–1 or 3–1 or 4–2, never decisive, seldom a clean sheet.

But if your team is doing well and you reach the play-offs, and the NASL pick a top American player of the season, the chances are they'll pick the goalkeeper. It was always odds-on the goalkeeper, because the best American players are natural goalkeepers, handling the ball far better than the outfield players can kick it.

In the Rowdies with me in 1976 we had Clyde Best, who was with West Ham, Mark Lindsay from Crystal Palace, Stewart Scullion, who is a Scot and played for Sheffield United and Watford, and then there were Stewart Jump, Derek Smethurst, all from England . . . and when we got to the play-offs the opposing goalkeepers were mostly Canadians, playing for Toronto, San Jose, Minnesota.

So they would insist on giving Arnie the big prize, which was worth about ten thousand dollars, although he was never worth that much – but he never had the brains to pass a few dollars around his American team-mates.

We tried to get a players' pool going over there, but the American players wouldn't have it, because they always insisted the English players were on more money anyway, which just wasn't true. We were only getting the same as we would have got in England – if we were gaining any extra, it was in experience.

But if American football hasn't yet got the traditions, it certainly has flair, and there are several things it could teach the English game. In this country you have the players, and then the management and the directors, and they seldom mix together. Outside you have the fans, and they can be completely divorced from what goes on inside the club, except on Saturday afternoons.

The Americans, on the other hand, try to involve the fans in the club as much as possible. They try to break down that exclusive clique barrier that exists so often over here. In Tampa we had news conferences every Monday, and afterwards the fans could stay on and have a spot of lunch with us. We would organize a talk-in with them, and I, as captain, would get up and say a few words, answer a few questions.

That way you got the feeling that the club belonged to everyone; everyone became involved.

Apart from the English players who were over in the States when I was – Bobby Moore, George Best, Mike England and the rest – Pele was still playing for New York Cosmos. In fact, we beat them 5–1 the first time we played them at Tampa, and then we were beaten 4–5 in the return at Dodgers Stadium, New York, in what they said was one of the best games ever seen in America at that time.

Incidentally, that was also one of the rare occasions I remember Arnie Mausser coming off his line, and he knocked me out, busted my lip. He went to punch the ball away, missed, and punched me instead!

Pele is a hell of a nice bloke and he's undoubtedly been the game's greatest ambassador in the States. His attitude to the game was unbelievable – he would eat, drink and sleep football. He'd be half-way across America promoting football one day and be back playing with Cosmos the next – he was their main asset.

I well remember going out for a meal with some friends from the Rowdies – there was Rowdies general manager, Beau Rogers, Lennie Glover and his wife, Susie and myself, and we went to Burns Restaurant in Tampa, one of the best in America, where the wine list is like a dictionary.

Anyway after the meal, the manager told us Pele was also there. It was a few days before we were due to play Cosmos and he'd come down for a soccer clinic and to do some VIP work. He was sitting with some friends and his personal manager, whom I recognized from the time I played for Team America.

Pele was terrific – so courteous. He kissed Susie on the cheek and really impressed her with his charm – and Susie's not impressed by footballers as a rule. But it just typified how good an ambassador he was.

Mind you, two days later, we still knocked hell out of him on the pitch. . . .

It helped the older stars from abroad like Pele and Beckenbauer and Eusebio to play on Astro-turf in the States. The game is played at a different pace – it slows everything down a shade, so you can appreciate ball-control and that. What you'd get in the side would be the younger players running off the ball, and the older stars receiving the passes and being allowed to sparkle with some immaculate control.

Those teams used to Astro-turf would go to Minnesota or somewhere and get absolutely hammered on grass, but to the average New Yorker, who's used to watching the game on Astro-turf and doesn't want to watch it any other way, it's a great spectacle.

They're actually building their own soccer stadiums now, too. Whereas in the early days they'd play on an adapted baseball ground or American football pitch, now they've got purpose-built grounds.

In this country you take a team like Watford, who've moved up from the Fourth to the Second – they're still stuck with basically a Fourth Division ground. In the States, if a club is successful they can move grounds. And if they hit a losing streak, they just cut their losses and move out again, no problems.

But then it's a whole different ball game over there. If you got an American over here watching Fourth Division football he'd probably not think much of it – because he's used to the very best. It's artificial in a lot of ways, but it's what they've got used to now.

Then again, travel is nothing to the Americans – they'll go hundreds of miles to see a good game. They'll go tail-gating, that is they'll throw a barbecue and the family in the car, drive to the ground, which probably has an enormous park close by, then get out the chairs and set up the barbecue. They get there, say, at one in the afternoon and the kick-off will be at eight in the evening, so they can make a family day of it. Mind you, they have so much more room than us, and better weather.

The American scene was good for me, because it kept me fit in the close-season, so I came back to Liverpool raring to go, and ready to get back my regular place in the side.

I was never tempted to stay in the States – that would have taken a lot of persuasion not only on me, but on Susie and the kids. It's all right for a few months, but I've still got my mum over here, and our friends, and business interests.

If I were starting to play again, though, I might be heavily tempted to go and spend a few years in the States, because there's no doubt so many English players find it's a better life out there altogether.

It can get quite ugly, though, and it does depend on what team you sign with. I was happy at Tampa, but when I went out again to Los Angeles Aztecs I saw the other side of the American game.

There is a tendency to treat footballers like commodities out there – you're just part of a cattle market. Advertising plays a big part in the game and you find you get asked to do a lot more than you would in this country. In England they're just happy if you play the game and play it well – in the States they want to make money out of you all the time.

Their transfer system is completely different from ours too; you can get one fellow who runs the club and decides who goes and who stays and you do what he tells you. I was a loan player so it didn't apply to me, but when I was at Los Angeles, as player-coach, which is their equivalent as manager, they sold Charlie Cooke without consulting me.

I had sold Georgie Best, and he probably deserved it – he

more or less sold himself because he wasn't trying a leg. He never bothered his behind, he was that disillusioned. But Charlie was a good player, and his attitude was right and he was an asset to the team. When I heard he was being asked to go I told him to sit tight until I'd sorted it out. But while I was on my way to see him he got ordered into the office to sign for another team.

I got really annoyed then and let off a bit of steam in the papers, told one or two home-truths, because there had been trouble in the team about cheques bouncing, and one or two other things. Several players had been sold as it happened – one was Ron Davies who used to play for Southampton and who was getting on a bit, although still a decent player – and I was getting the blame for it.

So I thought, sod it, I'm going to have a go, and I even went as far as taking a baseball bat with me to knock hell out of the Aztecs' boss Larry Friend, who went to ground when he heard I was on the warpath.

The management used to pay us on the last day of the month and the time we never made the play-offs most of the lads wanted to go home – it was the end of the season. I got a phone call to say the cheques would be available on the Saturday, the day most of us were leaving, and I could see us boarding our aeroplane clutching these cheques which would start bouncing in mid-air.

So I said, 'No way. The lads want their money now so they can cash the cheques while the banks are open. I've got a certain responsibility to these fellows and I want to see they get paid.'

So they brought the cheques round one afternoon fifteen minutes after the banks had closed. Next morning I went to cash mine early, and found some of the other lads there ahead of me. It all worked out in the end. But it was all so unnecessary. If the American game can teach us things like flair and communicating with the fans and sponsorship, I'm sure there's plenty we can teach them about management.

Larry Friend hired me to give him some advice, but he never listened to me. He made my job as coach difficult by insisting on selling players behind my back. In the end he made his team the laughing-stock of soccer in the States. It was a nightmare I was truly glad to be out of. I found it very worrying, very tiring.

The real trouble, I suppose, is this craving for instant success. It's taken a hundred years of football experience to bring the game to its present standard in this country. Americans, however, show a dangerous impatience for success, and are unforgiving if it isn't achieved.

At the same time, if English players realize there is a ready market for their skills in the States and the American clubs are patient and willing to build their own tradition, their own spectacle, then it can only be for the good of clubs on both sides of the Atlantic. You would have English clubs then being used as nurseries, if you like, for American soccer, and I don't mind that. Or more English players might end up playing in Europe, like Kevin Keegan. The international possibilities are exciting.

15 Bursting London's Pride

Liverpool have done so well in league and cup competitions in recent years that they've really become London's enemy. If a London club had done what Liverpool has done, they'd be putting up statues along the Mall by now.

I suppose what they feel is, to a certain extent, jealousy but then to read some of the national papers you often get the feeling there's nothing worth writing about north of Watford. They think we're all woolly-backs up north. This showed in the Ipswich and Arsenal FA Cup final, when Arsenal were built up so much in the press they felt the tension more than Ipswich, and were beaten. On the day, though, Ipswich were by far the better team.

It's the press in London who are to blame to a certain extent, but then it must be hard on them to have to write about second-class football. I suppose within the London area there must be eight or so League clubs, and only two or three with regular First Division places – like Arsenal, Chelsea and Tottenham, and even they are up and down like a fiddlers' elbow.

I still get quite a bit of fan mail, which is nice – but sometimes you get real idiots writing to you because of something you've said or something you've done to their favourite team or their favourite player.

I discard the vicious ones, those who are going to kill, those who call me 'King Rat', those who reckon I'm the biggest villain who ever wore a pair of football boots . . . but now and again when I get a sensible letter, I write one back.

I got quite a lot of mail over Malcolm MacDonald. I said in the *Liverpool Echo* that Malcolm loved shooting his mouth off, but didn't always match his words with his actions. No matter how hard he tried, he always seemed to end up with his boots stuck down his throat . . . Anyway, one of the London evening papers used a potted piece based on what I'd written and took lots of the phrases out of context, so the next thing I had was lots of irate letters from Arsenal supporters. One fellow even wrote and threatened to 'shute' me. I reckoned if his aim was as good as his spelling I had nothing to worry about.

But the sensible ones I replied to, giving the whole story, and I got a few back, saying, 'Thanks. We can understand it better now. We still don't agree with you, but at least we've got the whole picture.'

I still get letters of praise from southern supporters. If I did write slanging Arsenal, I might get a letter from a Spurs fan saying, 'Terrific, keep up the good work!'

I rarely get letters from up north, though. Not even from Manchester United or Leeds supporters. I used to get a few from Evertonians, but as Liverpool have got on top over the years, it's dropped to virtually nil. I've nothing against Evertonians, but unfortunately their team has been in the background of late. Two teams can't win the Championship, but their turn will probably come.

Certainly whenever I say anything about a southern player, or put a London club player on the deck, all hell's let loose. At Swansea we played QPR and I tackled Stan Bowles. Now because he's Stan Bowles, and because he decides to lie down, I get slated.

Foreign players coming over here and playing for London clubs took a long time to settle, too, because they just didn't fit in with the English manner of playing, and for many it was a hard lesson.

I got a lot of stick for tackling Ardiles when Swansea met Spurs in the League Cup competition. Match reporters said it was one of the worst tackles they'd seen since the bad old days of Norman Hunter, and my 'thigh-high tackle seemingly left Ardiles lying on Vetch Field like a wounded swan that had been blasted by a blunderbuss'.

It wasn't a bad tackle – it was a hard tackle, and the referee never booked me because it wasn't bad enough to warrant a booking. I think a lot of people, including Ardiles, just didn't expect it.

Spurs probably thought they'd set the English League alight when they bought him and his mate Villa. Because they'd won the World Cup, suddenly, overnight, the Argentinians were the greatest players ever – yet when they joined Spurs, first Swansea beat them 3–1 in the League Cup and then Liverpool battered them 7–0 at Anfield.

There was talk of Ardiles not playing for months after I tackled him, yet he was back for the return game. And even in the match in which I did tackle him – and the tackle was in the opening stages – he didn't go off till the seventieth minute, and that was a tactical move.

Villa got a bee in his bonnet about that tackle on his team-mate, though – he went over the ball probably more times than anyone in that match.

When you think how English managers often make big mistakes buying English stars, think how much greater the risk is in buying foreign stars and expecting them to adapt to the English game just like that.

I think a lot was expected of the Argentinians, but they mainly played like duds and have only recently started getting it together. Ardiles may be the nicest person in the game, but I don't think his impact has been that great. It all takes time.

There are players who don't look good but can get the most fantastic results; there are players who look average but can be vital members of any side because of their special skills . . . and then there are the players with bags of promise who fail to translate it into action. George Best is the classic example. I always got the impression George would die a young man with a big smile on his face. I saw a lot of him in America, and he always seemed to have no sense of responsibility at all. If playing football fell in with his plans for the day, then terrific . . . if not, you could never force him. But what a player! I've seen him do things instinctively in a game which would take other players their whole careers to try and accomplish. He's a nice bloke, terrific guy – but he's selfish and he doesn't give a hell. It's hard to get annoyed with a fellow like that.

Tony Currie, who was with Leeds and then joined QPR, was a lazy player, too. Tony was more an individualist; he'd do his own thing, and he wouldn't be motivated, which isn't a good thing when you're playing a team game.

Duncan McKenzie was a different player altogether. He looked good, he always tried, but he was never active enough, he never inspired confidence.

If you're talking about ball-control, they used to throw a penny to Ian St John, and he'd bring it down on his foot, flick it over his head, shoulder it, and watch it drop into his top pocket . . . Duncan had the same control. Give him lots of room and he looked magic – in the middle of the park. But once he got near goal and players started pressurizing him, he lost that sparkle.

I know I went to Goodison once and took quite a bit of stick from the Everton crowd because my choice of man of the match – this was a couple of years ago when I adjudicated a Cup match between Everton and Stoke – was Andy King. Andy was trying like hell, helping other players, creating chances, making things happen. The crowd, though, were captivated by Duncan, but although he looked good, did all the right things, his contribution to the game wasn't as busy as Andy's.

They used to say of Tony Hateley that he never bought a car, he bought a Pickford's van – they could have said the same of Duncan. I find it hard to believe that a truly great player needs to move around that often.

Ron Yeats organized our first players' pool at Anfield as far back as the 1965 Cup final, but because we didn't win much after that for a while, it died a bit of a death. We used to resent endless photographers turning up for the pre-season team photograph, then having the cheek to send us each a three-by-two with a note, 'If you want any more of these send 2/6 to me . . .'

The pool was resurrected around the 1971 Cup final when I took it over. We decided to arrange our own photographer and locked the freelancers and freeloaders out.

We soon realized there was a lot of cash to be made here, especially out of the photographs – everybody wanted photographs and we found out that the TV companies paid a copyright fee every time a player's picture appeared on the screen. So we got ourselves a contract with an agency and organized ourselves into a company with Stevie Heighway doing the books. We paid tax on the cash we received – it was all above board – but we just made it that little bit harder for photographers to exploit us.

There was nothing to stop them writing in and asking permission to take pictures of us training or something, but one time it was such a bore because it seemed everyone with a bit of a camera would be let into the training ground.

They'd be clicking away while we'd be training and it would take time for me to run over and say, 'Would you mind coming outside while I explain to you why you can't take pictures of us . . .' And then the trainer would shout over, 'You're supposed to be training. Get on with it!'

So, instead, I'd trade on my reputation and if there was a photographer there who shouldn't have been I'd run past and say, 'On your bike!' And next time round, 'You heard me. Fuck off!' and if he was still there, 'If you don't go by the time I'm back again, I'll give you a hiding.' And the fellows got the message by then.

It was remarkable the lengths they'd go to, though; rather than write in for permission to the club they'd get into someone's bedroom overlooking the ground. They'd rather slip some house-owner a couple of bob than do it properly.

Then when we'd go down to London for a game, when we ran out on to the pitch for the warm-up there'd be more photographers than players, so we'd pull a face, or turn our backs or thumb our nose – do something so they couldn't use it. We don't do it now, but at the time we resented them making a fortune out of us.

We began to organize one or two other things, too, like interviews at Cup final time. We never got into any bother with the papers at all and they began to find out I wasn't all that bad to deal with. Other teams now organize players' pools but Liverpool were the first. And we have no trouble – Stevie does the tax returns and it's all run right.

Sometimes things can get a bit on top of you – like the time we played St Etienne in the European Cup and we had to live with a film crew for about eight days. It got on your nerves every time you went out to find a bloody camera stuck up your nose. In the end it was a case of telling them to shift out and go home.

16 Bookings and Beatings

In my opinion, the worst tackle in the game is going over the ball, and I've never been booked for that. I have been booked for being a hard man and for swearing and only been sent off for dissent. On the other hand, I've been on the receiving end of some atrocious fouls, not only when I played for Liverpool but more especially when I joined Swansea. It is like a top-flight boxer used to fighting in top-flight halls having to settle for lesser dates; somehow one seems more vulnerable. There appeared to be more players ready to crock you, kick you when you're down. I became a natural target for those bruisers who like to boast in the pub of a Sunday, 'I did Tommy Smith yesterday . . .'

Some referees are like that, too. Give a lad a bad name and you're a natural target for their little book. Jack Taylor, over the years, booked me more than any other referee. I always got the impression he didn't like Liverpool, not just me in particular. But then referees and linesmen don't seem blessed with a sense of humour. Most referees suffer from being a 'homer', but some are more suspect than others. The worst ones may as well be wearing a red shirt one week and a claret one the next.

Basically I've always tried to ignore referees. As far as I'm concerned he's the man in black, and if he does his job right and blows his whistle at the right time, all well and good. But when he starts cocking things up, that's when he becomes the big ogre. And some of them can start acting like little Hitlers, and that's when they can spoil a potentially good game with their self-important antics.

Some referees, of course, stick in your mind. There was Roger Kirkpatrick – he was a bit of a showman and we used to call him Mr Pickwick. But then he disallowed a goal at the Arsenal and we lost the League on it – it was the last game of the season – thank God we never had him again after that.

Even Clive Thomas, for whom I have a lot of time, wasn't totally immune from the 'homer' instinct. I went over to him one game and said, 'You haven't given Liverpool anything all afternoon. It's about time you started.' I never swore at him, but I was persistent, and he sent me off.

The Jack Taylor thing began when he refereed the final of the Youth Cup between West Ham and Liverpool. We'd had a hell of a run, we weren't fancied but we'd reached the final, which was a two-legged affair, home and away. We'd won the home game 3-1, but lost the return something like 5–2. Our keeper, Swindlehurst, caught the ball, then their big chap Martin Britt whacked him into the back of the net, and Taylor gave a goal.

I got pretty excited – I was only seventeen – and threatened Taylor, said I'd batter him. After that he gave me the impression he singled me out.

One referee who used to stand out above everybody else, though, was Gordon Hill. He would enjoy a game as well as referee it, and if he made a mistake, he wasn't afraid to admit it.

Gordon was always fair – he would let the game flow and never blow up for trivialities. The biggest compliment you could pay him was to say you'd thought he'd gone home . . . he'd never interfere for the sake of making his presence known.

He also spoke the players' language and swore on the pitch, too, but it is a grown-up game and on the spur of the moment you're bound to let a few words fly. There was no hesitancy with Gordon, and he used to stick up for what he saw was right on the field. Lots of players would agree he stuck in their minds as a bloody good referee.

I'm afraid swearing on the pitch is part of the game anyway. If you get excited during a match, you're going to get into a situation where swearing is the obvious way to express yourself, where 'flipping' doesn't portray your mood that well, but a swear-word might!

We went through a phase of policemen booking players if they heard them swear from the touchline, but the fans swear too. Are they going to book thirty thousand excited people on the terraces? I agree that if a policeman hears someone swearing offensively outside the ground he's entitled to book them, but on the pitch swearing has become a way of life.

Bad language, too, is a part of everyday life, whether you like it or not, and people do get excited at football matches – almost as much as the players – so they are more likely to swear in the heat of the moment. It's a reflex action.

If people swear because it helps them let off steam. You're not going to stop them by asking them not to. And if other people get annoyed at football matches because some of those in the crowd start swearing, I'm afraid that's something they're going to have to get used to.

Trouble is that referees are not part of the football fraternity, they're not part of this exclusive club of football players. They did try, years ago, bringing referees round to clubs so they could talk together with players, but it wasn't successful.

It's probably time, though, that they did understand players better. At the moment they seem to want to treat you like kids – 'When I blow the whistle it's a foul, I want no arguing back, I want you ten yards away, no dissent, no swearing, just do as you're told like a nice little boy . . .'

They don't realize that the game is a player's livelihood. A referee could be marking exam papers the other side of England the night before a game and when he applies for a passport he writes 'teacher' or 'shop assistant' or whatever; for a footballer, the game is a way of life and he puts his profession down as 'professional footballer'.

I think the day must come when there are professional referees. Think of the number of players who finish early or who come to the end of their playing days and want to be associated with the game: there's a limit to the number of managers and coaches jobs they can fill. If the League put them through a course to turn them into professional referees the game could only benefit.

Mind you, it's probably a bit like asking a professional driver to become a traffic warden, but at least they'd understand players a bit more. And they should go round in packs of three so that if the referee gets injured another qualified man can take his place instead of the linesman or someone from out of the crowd running the line. That only leads to more 'homer' decisions.

Homers are quite common really. It's the reason why a team at the bottom of the division can seemingly beat Liverpool at their ground against all the odds. It's only because the referee has allowed himself to be influenced by the crowd or whatever and he's giving free kicks, throw-ins, everything to them.

Admittedly it's a hard job, but a professional referee doing it for a decent wage should be able to make a better job of it.

Contrary to what many people think, there's never any needle in a game before it starts; there may be tension, of course, built up by the press and that, and some players may get out on the park a bit nervous, a bit uptight, but that's all.

Where there's real tension is the Wembley occasion, like Cup finals. We won the Cup in 1965 and lost it in 1971, but it wasn't until we got to Wembley in 1974 and battered Newcastle that we really played well there.

The Charity Shield game in 1974, when we played Leeds at Wembley, was a bit of a shambles – Bremner and Keegan were sent off, and I got booked along with Johnny Giles. But the person who started it all never got a mention, and that was Allan Clarke. On the pitch he's like an arsonist – he sparks off the blaze, then retires to a safe distance to watch the fire.

As soon as we started the game Clarke went over the ball to Phil Thompson, and when I say went over the ball he could have broken his leg. But he wasn't pulled up for it. Then later in the first half I went in on Clarke hard, and I got booked. So by half-time there was more than a bit of needle in the game.

Into the second half and we were winning 1–0, then first Giles and then Bremner fouled Keegan. The whole thing developed into a bit of a shindig and the ref booked Giles and sent Kevin and Billy off. Why in the world Kevin took his jersey off I don't know – I don't think he knows either – and Bremner took his off as well. Anyway the game developed into a bit of an anti-climax after that. It was 1–1 at full-time and it was the first time it had to be decided on penalties. We won on the spot kicks.

Of course there was an FA inquiry and myself, Giles, Keegan and Bremner had to go up. Kevin and Bremner got a month's ban and were fined £500, then Johnny and I went in. The chairman starts off, 'Right, you've been charged with bringing the game into disrepute . . .' And I'd only been booked!

And he points a finger at me and says, 'You started all this.' Now disciplinary hearings can be a bit nerve-wracking but I'd been to a couple so I wasn't that bad, and I got up and said, 'Excuse me, but I didn't start it.'

Anyway he starts ranting on about 'You footballers, you get too much money' and all that sort of thing, right off the subject. Sir Matt Busby was on the panel, too, and he came in with, 'Well, we all know Tommy tackles hard, and it's just one of those things.'

In the end all they did was record it and left it at that for both of us. But like I said, we wouldn't have been there if it hadn't been for Allan Clarke. He was one of a breed – he started the aggro in that Wembley match, no doubt about it, yet he never got done for it.

But then there are disciplinary committees and disciplinary committees. I remember I got done for accumulating points when I was on the verge of getting my England cap, and playing in the Under-23s, and Shanks came with me to the hearing and said, 'You'll get off today.' I said 'Why?' He said, 'You're playing in the Under-23s. I'm telling you, you'll get off. They don't want to suspend players who could play for England.'

I took it with a pinch of salt, but when we got there I did get off. I was just warned as to my future conduct and that was it. I was so relieved I got up and shook hands with the three fellows behind the desk, with Shanks pulling my sleeve and hissing, 'Come on, get out before they change their minds. . . .'

17 Adopt a Club a Day

I think it's pretty clear that there must be changes in the English game in the near future if it is to survive. But, sadly, I believe the biggest bugbear to the sport at the moment is the Football League itself.

They would appear to be putting more restrictions on English football than anyone else. Sponsorship and the flow of extra cash into the game can do nothing but good – I'm sure the average footballer doesn't care where the cash comes from so long as he gets a decent wage. I don't even think he'd mind taking part in the coaching clinics set up by his club during the summer to keep the youngsters interested. These clinics are a great success in the States, and are a good way of bringing the players closer to the public. What clinics there are in this country at the moment are sponsored by private firms – if the clubs could organize their own it would be a good way of spotting potential talent and keeping youngsters interested in their own club, by showing an interest in them.

More clubs, too, ought to be able to apply for sponsorship, because with transfer fees and wages rising so quickly, unless new ideas are accepted soon there's not that many clubs that are going to be able to survive.

It would be a nice idea if clubs in the First Division were able to adopt clubs in the lower divisions, to ensure their survival and treat them as nurseries for their own future players. It would also be nice if leagues were organized on a regional basis, as they also do in the States to cut down the travelling expenses, with play-offs at the end of the season. At the moment none of this is entirely feasible in this country, with our cup competitions and suchlike, but I would at least like to see it discussed.

I'm also for keeping football a poor man's sport, keeping the admission price down to bring in the big crowds, and we can do that only by attracting more money into the game from other sources. We have to be fair to our fans, but the Football League restrictions, and indeed their whole attitude to reasonable change, appears to be stifling the English game.

Take shared stadiums. It's ludicrous to have ninety-odd clubs in the English League all with their own grounds and half of them with turn-of-the-century facilities. Some grounds are a real disgrace, but the money available for a face-lift could mean a lick of paint to cover the cracks, or a new length of plumbing to stop the stand leaking. Some of the toilets probably haven't been modernized since Victoria died.

Traditional rivalries will always exist, but I can't see them running that deep that they mean Liverpool and Everton, or even Celtic and Rangers, can't share a modern stadium with modern facilities. And those who stay away because it is a shared stadium, shared with their traditional 'enemies', will be far outnumbered by those who will come because it's a modern ground.

It should be possible for these stadiums to be all-seat affairs too. People say all-seat stadiums will cut down the number of fans who can watch the game – well, what's the use of having a stadium that holds 60,000, with 20,000 seated and 40,000 standing if only 40,000 turn up each week. Better to have 40,000 all-seats and fill it every week.

I would also like to see football played in the summer to encourage more families to come. It would beat the winter weather too – at the moment we can come to the end of a season with a terrific backlog of games because of snow, icy pitches, and the like.

Far better to start the season around February or March and let it flow through until September. It would give fans a chance of seeing better football on greener pitches, and the summer sun would probably discourage violence too. The louts come to the games in the winter only because there's nothing else to do. There's a lot more distractions in the summer, and its warmer too, which seems to take the heat out of fighting gangs.

I know from watching horseracing that no horse is keen to race when it's damp or windy, but give him a bit of sun on his back and he'll run all day. I know what sort of conditions I would rather play football in – I'd far rather stroke a ball around on a green and grassy pitch than try and kick it through an inch of snow.

It would also give the players a chance to take a winter break as well. At the moment they don't get a summer holiday with their families. You stop playing football when your children are still at school, then when they break up for the summer you're back in training for the next season. So unless you take your children away from school for a few weeks you can't have a holiday with your family.

As for Christmas, you may as well forget that, too, at the moment. In our house, unless the weather was really bad, for many years the drill was for me to get up, have a spot of breakfast with the family, give them their presents, get changed and go to work.

And then people also say, well you haven't got to do it all your life, only till you're thirty-five or so. Well, that's what I've done . . . and now my children are teenagers and perhaps don't want to come on holiday with me any more. It sometimes seems as though they've grown up without my noticing them. It's one of those sacrifices every player has to make – it's selfish too, because we enjoy playing football – but now and then it would be nice to spend a holiday with the family at a reasonable time of the year.

We must be able to sort our seasons out better than this. The way things are at the moment you virtually need a whole new rule book. Take the points system – in the States they have evolved a system where clubs get points for goals. In this country, if you get beat 4–0 or 5–4 you still come away with nothing and your opponents get two points for a win. Under the American system the losers can still get points for the goals they score up to a maximum of three and the winners get three points, plus bonus points for their goals up to a maximum of three. So if you lost 5–4 you'd at least come away with three points, while your opponents would get six. And this keeps the interest alive till the last game of the season.

The only thing wrong with the American system is that it makes no allowance for draws – they have what they call overtime and then shoot-outs to decide a winner. It's a points system that's needed over there to add interest in the game, though when they enter international competitions they have to revert to the points system we use.

It's all right being a revolutionary, but there's no guarantee the Football League are going to listen to anybody. Their attitude seems to be, 'We're English. We invented the game. We've always done it this way . . .' To them the rules are like the Ten Commandments, not to be broken, and certainly never to be altered.

It all boils down to tradition – but I'm afraid if the League wants maybe five or six clubs to go to the wall because of tradition, it's barking up the wrong tree. English football needs sponsorship to survive.

I accept that your team colours are sacred, but I can't see anything wrong with putting the Co-op across your back. It's not going to affect the way you play.

I know Liverpool are able to attract the big sponsors, like Hitachi (even though they can't wear their sponsor shirts on Match of the Day) but I'm also sure that smaller clubs can work out some sort of deal with smaller, local sponsors. Like Tranmere could maybe get Joe Bloggs' Diner to sponsor them for five or six weeks at a time – it can only be good for the game.

What is worrying, I suppose, is that foreign firms are showing British firms the way in this regard – maybe they have more money to splash around, but British firms have also mostly been hidebound by tradition, wary of pushing themselves forward. Foreign firms seem to have the confidence that some British firms lack.

Sponsorship isn't the only change you can make to a player's shirt – take the numbering system as well. We number our players from one to eleven, based on an old-fashioned lay-out of team positions. Now in training at Anfield, you're given a number when you join the club and you keep it until you leave. I was always no. 28, and I knew immediately which were my boots, or if someone else had my tracksuit on. It's also more hygienic that way – to know which is your kit and to stick to it.

If we adopted this numbering system and carried it over on to the pitch on Saturdays – like they do in the States – fans would get to know your number and know if you were playing that afternoon or not, without having to catch a mumbled tannoy announcement like, 'Wearing the no. 4 shirt today is . . .'

You wouldn't need to print so many thousand different programmes each week either. You would be able to slip that week's team as an insert sheet into the club magazine – it would save a lot of money.

It all seems pretty simple to me – like the kit itself. The suppliers' emblems on the kit you wear on Saturdays are a load of kiddology anyway. To my mind Adidas is probably the best boot around, because the firm have been at it longer than most of the others, so if your team is tied down to another supplier and you can't get on with their boots – I've seen boots in production in America which are eighth-class let alone second-class – you simply take your Adidas boots and change the stripes. Then your team sponsor is happy, you're happy because you feel more comfortable and you'll play a good game.

It's hard to think of ways to deter the louts who come to football matches, but maybe if clubs encouraged more of a family atmosphere at their grounds it would help. So would stiffer sentences for offenders.

At the moment, with grounds tightly packed with people, and a lack of other things to do on wet and windy Saturday afternoons in winter, it's no wonder fights break out. Plus the fact that the press and television lads build up the conflict before a game . . . if a lout and his gang know they can make front-page news tomorrow they're going to hit someone over the head with an iron bar or a bottle, to get themselves in the paper. Maybe if they were ignored, they'd lose interest.

I also think professional referees would stop some of the violence, too, which is often sparked off by a bad decision. A spot of real authority on the pitch might earn a bit more respect on the terraces.

Mind you, violence at football matches hasn't just started. It's been going on for years, but it's never been much publicized till recently. It's all part of the sick society we live in – we seem to like seeing people's heads get kicked in, or so you'd think to watch the news.

Violence on the pitch, though, has petered out a lot in the past ten years. They used to say stamp out the violence on the pitch and you'll stamp out the violence on the terraces, but that was never true.

I don't mind barriers going up to stop the fans getting on to the pitch – when you're out there playing you feel like you're in a goldfish bowl anyway. Barriers are only to comply with FIFA rules, because they are more frightened of violence on the Continent than we are. It's much worse in other countries – I mean they still shoot referees in South America!

They blame soccer, too, for all the graffiti you see over the walls these days, but I think if anything's successful, people are going to shout about it. Fifteen years ago the walls in Liverpool were covered with Beatles slogans. People have always written over the walls.

The fellow who thought of putting up a placard in public toilets for people to write on had the best idea. Instead of writing all over the walls you write on it and when it's full they either paint over it or give you a new one and you start again.

If people feel the urge to write on walls, then give them a wall to write on. They do it on the Continent and it's a great success.

And then again, if you get louts going to a football match and all they really want to do is fight, provide them with an open field in the middle of nowhere, with a fleet of ambulances round the outside, and tell them, 'If you want to knock hell out of each other, do it there. But don't involve other people.'

At the end of it, they're probably going to turn round and say 'What the hell are we doing? There are all those folk enjoying a good game of football and we've ended up with broken bones and bloody noses. That can't be right. . . .'

I don't really think the violence has that much to do with football – we tried to segregate the fans, but all they did was fight outside the ground.

So make sentences stiffer, make fines greater – and if that stops it, great, but if it doesn't I don't think you can blame the football clubs. What goes on outside the grounds isn't their concern.

18 Fast Ladies, Furious Fights

Footballers do belong to an exclusive club, with its own code and its own in-jokes. It's hard for a newcomer to be accepted right away; the best thing to do is keep your mouth shut, watch your step and bide your time.

In my early days, at LFC's Christmas dinner the older players would ask the newcomers and the groundstaff lads to get up and give a bit of a song – I remember we did 'Ten Green Bottles', which had to be the funniest thing you ever heard. But sometimes initiations can be rougher – it all depends on the victim.

We used to go to Majorca every year with the team and play these impromptu games of 'football tennis' on the beach. In fact, they used to frown on just anybody playing ball-games on the beach, but because we were Liverpool FC we could get away with it, and we used to attract quite a crowd.

Well, we'd been going there a couple of seasons when Phil Boersma joined Liverpool and came with us. It was a sweltering afternoon and we'd taken a break in a pub when Phil rides by on a bike with this bird. Well it was the sort of day when it would have been hard to raise a trot, let alone go for a bike ride.

He got his leg pulled over that, and being young and cocky he got a little niggled. So the next night we said, 'Come out for a drink with us,' knowing that in the back of his mind he had the idea he could drink as much as anybody.

So we took him to a bar we knew, and we asked the lad behind the bar to lace the drinks. We were drinking small Bacardis with lots of Coke while Phil was into the triple vodkas and what-have-you, with a little tonic.

By half-past ten he was flat out on the floor, so we carried him back to the hotel and into his room, stripped him off, put bootpolish on his private parts, stuffed toothpaste up his ass and smeared him all over with Nivea cream.

Then we threw him in bed with everything we could find in the room, and left him there with the wardrobe on top of him. When he emerged about two days later he was a different lad. And to this day he can't stand the smell of Nivea – it makes him ill.

But then Phil was only young and cocky with it – to a certain extent he was asking for it. After that he was one of the lads, terrific guy.

I can also remember Gordon Milne one night out drinking Cointreau with Reuben Bennett – large measures and he wasn't used to it. 'Just like lemonade,' he was saying.

He had to be carried back and it took two or three days to put his stomach right. He was really ill – and we used to pop in to cheer him up and say, 'All right, Gordon? Fancy a greasy bacon butty?' And he'd be off down to the toilet again!

But then it had always been a tradition to play hard and relax hard if you like. Everybody would let off a bit of steam after a game. I remember an early reserves game when I hadn't been there long and we were playing Newcastle, staying overnight in some hotel. Alfie Arrowsmith comes down to breakfast the next morning with a shocking headache.

So the lads say, 'A couple of Alka-Seltzer, Alfie, that's what you need. You'll soon be okay.' So they give him these Alka-Seltzer and he says, 'I've never taken these before. What do I do with them?' So we say, 'Oh, stick 'em in your coffee.'

We were taking coffee in the lounge so he lobs these two tablets into his cup . . . in no time at all the table's covered in brown froth, and he's sitting there, not sure what to do, trying to shovel it up in his hands and put it back in the cup. And everybody just got up and pretended he wasn't with us.

The funniest things do seem to happen abroad. Footballers, like anybody else, like to relax with a bit of light reading when they're travelling, and on most of our away games you'd get one of the lads buying *Penthouse*, another *Club International*, and someone would get *Playboy* and they'd get passed around.

But Brian Hall was that mad on cars he used to buy *Motor Sport*, *Autocar*, that sort of thing. One time we were playing in Germany in a UEFA Cup-tie and staying outside of town in an hotel. After the game Cally and myself and one or two others stayed in for a drink, while Brian and some of the other lads went back into town for a drink at a club.

When they came out to return to the hotel a beautiful Mercedes sports-car turns up with a gorgeous bird at the wheel, and she leans over and invites Brian to take a ride. Well, Hally's so enthralled with the car he doesn't work it out very fast, and gets in. They're away down the road when it begins to dawn on him what her game is, and then he decides he doesn't want to know. But by the time she lets him out he's completely lost – doesn't know where the hell he is, can't remember the name of our hotel and ends up having to go to the local police station. They make a few inquiries and bring Brian back to us in a police car!

Big Ronnie Yeats and I went to Majorca for a holiday with Liverpool when I was only a raw lad. I'd gone out for a few drinks to a little club with Gerry Byrne and Reuben Bennett, and there was a German lad there who started getting a bit nasty, so we buggered him off. Then the Spanish barman took the German's side and threw us out after an argument.

We got back to the hotel about the same time as Ron Yeats was getting out of a taxi and we said, 'Hey, Ron, there's this lad in this club who's turned out a bit naughty . . .' He got back in the taxi with me and we went back to the club.

The manager appeared when we got back, and the barman was still spoiling for a fight. So I said to the manager, 'I've been insulted by your barman and insulted by your doorman and I don't think it's right.' (Not in those words, but something like that . . .)

And the manager was saying, 'Get out. Closed.' And we were

saying, 'No. Apologize.' The next thing was, he pulled out a gun. So I looked at Ron and he looked at me and we backed out the door. At which the doorman got a bit brave again and slammed it in our faces.

Ronnie had a real cob on by then, so he put his foot to the door, gave it a kick; it flew open and there was the barman standing there, the full height of him. Ronnie just went 'pop' on his nose, and down he went.

Then the manager and the doorman are throwing all the small Spanish waiters out into the courtyard at us. Chairs were being thrown about and tables breaking. Those waiters were coming out of the concrete like a swarm of locusts. But you had only to hit them once and they stayed down.

Finally, we heard a siren in the distance, so we turned round and legged it. Next morning I said to Ronnie, 'He had a gun, you know,' and Ronnie said, 'I know!' And we both realized how scared we'd been.

We were playing in Sweden at one time, and relaxing in our hotel room, when Jack Whitham came bursting in and said, 'I've done it! I've done it!'

We looked at each other and asked, 'What's that, Jack?'

'I've hit that doorman. He was being funny to me, just once too often. I'd had enough of him so I laid one on him.'

We told him he'd better watch it, because the doorman would probably go to the police.

'I don't care,' he said. 'He was asking for it.'

He went off to his room and we looked over the landing to see the doorman – who'd obviously forgotten all about it. He just sat there reading a book.

We left Jack for a while, then Ron Yeats and myself went across to his room and knocked on the door. Jack was rooming with Kevin Keegan. Kevin opened the door, and cottoned on quickly. . . .

'What do you want?' he said.

In his best foreign accent Yeatsie said, 'You Jack Whitham?'

Kevin said, 'Oh no. He's not here.'

We said, 'We have to search room. . . .'

In the end we burst into the room, trying to keep a straight face, with Kevin playing along. Jack was in the bathroom, pressed against the wall just like a fly and trying to hide behind the shower curtain. He was terrified – he really thought we were the police.

19 Swansea Twilight

I'll always be grateful to Swansea for having faith in me, to Tosh for giving me a three-year contract when Liverpool only wanted to give me a one-year. It started out as purely a business transaction. I'm in a pension scheme that guarantees you a sum when you stop playing, but you have to play till you're thirty-five. Liverpool's contract meant I would be playing till I was thirty-four and then have the trouble of maybe finding another club to take me over the deadline.

Tosh offered me a three-year contract which took me well over the limit. All I really wanted to do was play. I had never given much thought to playing anywhere else but Liverpool, and in the first place I suppose it was for selfish reasons that I went to Swansea.

But when I got there I had a surprise. First and foremost I found out Swansea wasn't just the small mining village I suppose most northerners think it is – it's quite a big place, and attractive, and they are interested in football; some good players have come from round there, like the Charles brothers and the Allchurches.

What they probably wanted was an injection of something to keep the interest alive and give them a boost, and Tosh felt maybe one or two of the older Liverpool players might be all right for them, such as myself and Cally, Alan Waddle and Phil Boersma. He asked me to go there, if you like, to do him a favour, and he didn't restrict me by asking me to go there and live. I could still train at Liverpool and travel to the games, so in fact I was getting the best of both worlds.

And don't forget we were only a Third Division club then, and Tosh was still playing. And when we drew Tottenham in the League Cup we got twenty-five to thirty thousand people along to see us. The average gate for that season was probably around fourteen thousand, a lot more than some Second Division clubs.

I was surprised to find there were other places with just as avid football supporters as Liverpool. And Tosh has got a grip on the place, by transforming it into a little bit of Liverpool, reorganizing one or two things along Anfield lines.

I could have gone to other teams – I could have gone to Walsall or Hereford, or even Tranmere, but that would have meant staying too much in the shadow of Liverpool, and I didn't want to do that. Actually being involved with a successful side with one or two promising players coming along, like Robbie James and Jeremy Charles, who is Mel Charles's son, well, I think Cally and I chose right.

They're probably never going to reach the same heights as Liverpool, but the atmosphere is good and people do get excited about the game. Some grounds you go to and people turn up because it's the sociable thing to do, others you go to and people turn up to knock hell out of each other. I get excited about football because it's an exciting sport, and I like people who get excited about the game, the same way as I do. They do that at Swansea. But I did miss that professional First Division attitude to the game.

At Anfield my weaknesses were known to every other player on the park, and I knew their weaknesses, and you'd try to cover for them the way others would try and cover for me.

In the Third Division, players subconsciously seem to be playing for themselves and not for others. A team is only as good as its strengths and weaknesses, and so long as you use some of your strength to cover for others' weaknesses you'll be all right. If you don't you start to struggle.

Some of the players maybe haven't come to terms with

gaining promotion in successive seasons from the Fourth to the Second Divisions. Perhaps it's happened that fast it hasn't registered with them. But it disappoints me sometimes that players don't get excited at the prospects that have opened up for them.

Basically they're still Fourth Division players in some of their attitudes, but as Tosh develops their confidence it will come. It just hasn't sunk in yet.

One of the things you learnt at Liverpool was that you rarely make the same mistake twice. I don't think other clubs concentrate on mistakes and learning from them as much as Liverpool do, but it all comes back to the weaknesses and strengths thing, and it can all be ironed out in training.

The way you train is different from the way you play. I didn't go round getting stuck in in the five-a-sides like I would on a Saturday. Most of the Liverpool players knew my weakness was that I could never sprint that quickly. Ask me to run a marathon and I would probably have a chance – I can keep going all day – but ask me to do a hundred metres and I might as well pack it in on the starting line.

So at Swansea, and at other lower division clubs, I would say the greatest thing to learn is the other fellow's weakness – and concentration. That's the key to today's game.

When we were kids in training at Melwood with Shanks playing five-a-side, and the ball went behind the goal, two of us would go, one to fetch it and the other to back up, so that the one who fetched it could flick it to his mate and to a certain extent the rhythm of the game wouldn't be interrupted.

At Swansea I'd see the ball go behind the goal. One goes to get it and all the rest start running away up the other end of the park to wait for the kick. There's nobody running alongside anybody else to give that bit of support.

Some players tend to watch the game, too, rather than take part in it. Linesmen do it as well – if the ball's not in their part of the park they'll spectate – 'Oh that's a good ball . . .' – then when it comes their way they're not expecting it. That's why some decisions are late, and why some good build-ups fall down.

We were taught so well as kids that today we do a lot of things automatically, a lot of moves we just take for granted. You have to teach a player to think for himself. Whether you're the biggest star or the youngest player you've got a place in that team, and the older players should help the younger ones develop their own talents, and use their initiative.

At Liverpool they made you proud to belong to the club, and I can see the same attitude coming at Swansea. The lads are gaining confidence, the atmosphere is good. What they have to do is maintain that atmosphere and build on that confidence when the pressures start being put on them in the higher divisions.

It's all too easy to think, 'We've done it, we've got promotion' and do nothing about it, or think that's the end of it. It's really only the beginning – and you have to start all over again if you're going to stay up and play in the bigger leagues.

There are some teams who are just content to stay middle of the table year after year, and they start panicking only when the old thumbscrews begin turning and it looks like they're in danger of going down. A good team takes enjoyment from winning, learns from losing and is able to live with the pressures of success when it comes.

Swansea is under pressure now – they've got to be good, they've got to be the Swansea of tomorrow. And I think they'll make it.

One of the main things Liverpool did for me over the years was push my confidence forward. As a kid I was a shy lad, believe it or not. They put confidence in me to try and put confidence in everyone else.

At Swansea, when I talked to the lads about football, I always emphasized that the biggest thing these days is concentration. Shouting the game is becoming more and more important too, letting everyone on your side know what you're going to do, and what you're not going to do, making them go left, making them go right. In the First Division, shouting the game is, say, twenty-five per cent of the action; in the Third Division it's maybe five per cent, because the game's not as cultured as the First.

In the Third Division everyone tends to watch the ball, and run after it. If you like, they never grow up, because children always watch the ball and run after the ball. It's still football, but it's different from the First Division where people shout because they're confident, telling somebody to do something, go somewhere. Perhaps one out of ten shouts may be wrong, but you overlap that with nine out of ten shouts being good, so nobody says anything to you. Then in the Third Division nobody shouts, everyone follows the ball, something happens and you were maybe in a position to prevent it, and you say, 'Why didn't you give me a call?'

One of the things about being captain of any side is you have to be able to give the others enough confidence to get through even when you're playing badly. I've had many a bad game, but the team's played all right because I've countered that by shouting the game, and keeping them going.

You don't want people coming up to you and saying, 'Hey, you're not saying much today! Are you having a bad time?' I think that's where Liverpool to a certain extent have toppled everybody else – sheer confidence.

20 Home and Away

I think what fascinated me about my wife Susie first of all was the fact that her family took absolutely no interest in football.

Being on the groundstaff at Anfield at the time was the big 'in' with all the birds – added to which I firmly believed that everyone in Liverpool either worshipped at Anfield or Goodison Park. It could be a bit of a bind, though – you'd go out with a bird, and the next thing was her father, and all her brothers, and her cousins twice removed were queuing up and pestering you for tickets to the match.

I suppose if Susie's father and family had been the same I might have gone off her as well; as it was, we met through a friend, Mick Kelly, who invited me out one night on a blind date to make up a foursome. His current girlfriend, Sandra, was Susie's friend, and we ended up going to the Locarno together.

I was sixteen then and it was a year after my dad died. He had been quite strict with me – I had to be in at a certain hour, say nine o'clock, and I had to do my homework and bits and bats around the house before I went out.

When he died things changed – I still did my chores, because there was no way I was going to take advantage of Mum, but I certainly found myself staying out later.

Nights out with my mates were something I wouldn't have been keen on when Dad was alive, but now I was a breadwinner in the family, Mum probably thought I was more grown up and responsible . . . she had the nous not to restrict me and let me get on with my life.

So, at fifteen, with a couple of bob in my pocket from Liverpool FC, I started taking girls out, going to the pictures, that sort of thing.

I remember Mick and I took two birds home one day – they lived down by Everton Brow and we were supposed to be helping them babysit. Once in the house there was a couch and a chair, so we tossed for it, and Mick won the couch. I sat in the chair with this bird on my lap.

So there we were all cosy, watching telly, and having a kiss and a cuddle – the baby was as good as gold, didn't wake up at all – when we heard the key in the door, and the parents coming home.

The bird I was with got up to introduce me when they walked into the room, and I got up . . . and fell over. She must have been sitting on a muscle in my leg, because it went completely dead. I was up and down all in one go, feeling dead embarrassed about it, sprawled on the rug.

But even then, when she told her father I was on the ground-staff at Anfield, he was quite impressed. He was prepared to forgive me anything for that – and while he was about it, did I happen to have a ticket for . . .

Anyway, I was sixteen when I met Susie, and we saw a lot of each other after that. We eventually got married when I was nineteen – on 4 July 1964.

Footballers tend to think in seasons and games rather than years – and it's hopeless when I try to remember my kids' birthdays (at least that's my excuse).

Ask me when Darren was born, and I'll say 1965 Cup final, because it immediately rings a bell that Susie didn't go to the game because she was expecting, and the next month Liverpool were off to Majorca for a holiday, but I had to miss the trip when Susie went into hospital. Darren was, in fact, born that June and I used to pull Susie's leg about her timing because it meant I missed a holiday with the lads.

Janette I associate with Christmas, mainly because Susie was ill that time, and Janette was born in the January, when we got beat by Ferencvacos 1–0. That was the 1967–8 season . . .

When we were first married we had a club house on Northway, Maghull, just outside Liverpool, next door to Phil Chisnell. Ron Yeats lived round the corner and I used to rely on him to give me a lift into the ground on match days. One day, of course, he forgot. I was sitting in the bay window waiting for him when I saw his car go steaming past, so I had to cop a taxi and try and make it in time. I think I got to the ground with about ten minutes to spare.

Big Ron thought it was a huge joke – he'd just been day-dreaming and forgot all about me.

My son Darren, who's fifteen now, likes his football, but he also likes tennis, badminton, squash, any sport really, which is a good thing, so long as he gets enough exercise. He's at college now where they play rugby, but I don't think he's taken to it, mainly because we've never been a rugby family. Basically I just let him go his own way, so long as he gets his homework done and works hard at school. The one thing he does seem to excel in is art.

Janette has taken to gymnastics, and if anything she tends not to worry so much as Darren. Nothing much seems to worry her; it's like water off a duck's back. Darren takes in what's happening around him, but Janette can take it or leave it. Janette and Darren enjoy life and get on well together; they've probably had it a bit easier than I did and if they lack anything it's that little bit of hardness to the outside world that comes with having to fight for what you want.

I'm naturally proud of both my children, but I used to find myself thinking of Darren when I was on the pitch. During a game, if one of the other team made a mess of it, I'd say, 'Bloody hell, I've a son at home who can head a ball better than you!' And in some cases it was true.

It frightens me sometimes to realize I can go anywhere in the country and someone will recognize me. I can go strolling through the smallest village and be stopped by someone. It alarms me at times to find I have no privacy. That's why I built a wall around my place after we got back from Rome – to save me from the nosey parkers. I can't think why people should want to peer into my garden just to look at Tommy Smith. If Sophia

Loren were living next door to me, I could understand it, but me. . . !

It also amazes me to realize what Liverpool have won. They've won more since 1961, when they got back in the First Division, than they did in the previous seventy-odd years of their history. It's frightening to think one team could get such a wealth of talent under one roof and keep it. Nobody else has been able to do it with such success, such consistency.

As a kid I used to think of Real Madrid as the greatest thing since sliced bread – they were the top European team – now people talk about Real Madrid and Liverpool in the same breath. Barcelona used to be the other team you spoke about with Real Madrid – now people in Barcelona talk about Liverpool. Barcelona are just another team now. It's unbelievable the way Liverpool have achieved the right to stand on the same pedestal as Bayern Munich and Real Madrid.

At times it seems the only thing European soccer has taught us is the way to win the European Cup . . . it took British teams five years or so to get used to the European game, to prepare properly for the European game, to play the European game.

But it's got to the point where they can't teach us anything now. We used to look to them for skills, but they've never been able to match us for stamina. And the other thing they've got to learn from us now is how to score goals with their heads.

I had no idea whatsoever that I was in line for any sort of honour, and it still amazes me to think that I should have been singled out for services to sport, but after we got back from Rome, I found myself being approached to see if I'd accept an MBE.

For a long while I thought it was a joke that the lads were pulling on me, something that I thought Jimmy Tarbuck was in on.

At the reception at the Walker Art Gallery, the Liverpool FC secretary, Peter Robinson, said to me, 'The Prime Minister's going to phone you sometime soon.' And we'd been celebrating, we'd been drinking, so I just said, 'Oh yeah . . .' but didn't take it in. There were a lot of jokes going around that night, that even when Peter did try to explain it to me I still didn't believe it.

So I completely forgot all about it; my testimonial came round later in the week and I stayed the night on the Friday at the Holiday Inn in Liverpool. After the game we'd got stuck into the champagne and had a meal, and I was in bed by maybe ten-thirty or so, when the telephone went.

And this posh voice on the other end said, 'Are you still all right to see me downstairs in reception at eleven?' And it dawned on me through a slightly drunken haze that someone had telephoned earlier and said they'd be calling in later.

Now at the time, Jimmy Tarbuck and Kenny Lynch were also staying at the hotel, and when they get together, well anything can happen. So I thought, 'Aye, aye, Tarby's having me on. He's got Kenny to ring up, put on a posh voice and the pair of these nutters are going to have me running round this hotel like Soft Joe.'

I was still suspicious when I got dressed and went down to reception about ten to eleven and found Tarby there, and he said, 'I'm just going out for a while.' I thought he's just going out to be at a safe distance and watch me looking for this non-existent chap with a posh voice.

But at the same time I could also see this little fellow by the desk and the girl behind the desk is pointing in my direction. So I went over and he said, 'Mr Smith, can I have a word . . . I've been empowered by Her Majesty . . . please keep it confidential . . . you've been selected for an MBE. . . .' And I'm sitting there waiting for the punchline, for the big mickey-take. It still didn't register. I suppose it was only when the papers arrived that I realized it was for real.

I think Susie was more excited than me for a long while, and when the Birthday Honours list was published I was in Hawaii, touring with Bobby Charlton's All-Star team. That was funny, because Bobby and his brother Jack both had OBEs, Cally was with us and he'd also got an MBE. In the same list they awarded Bob Paisley an OBE – following Shanks because he had an OBE too.

When I went to the Palace for the investiture we got a friend to provide a Rolls for us and I took Susie and the children along. The same day as I was there, Roger Taylor and J. P. R. Williams were also at the Palace to pick up awards, and what impressed me first of all was that the gathering was not all upper-class lords and ladies but ordinary folk, all waiting to meet the Queen. And one of the first people to come up to me was a lady from Southampton – I think she was a teacher – who said, 'When I knew I was to be here on the same day as you, all the kids said I had to bring back your autograph,' – so I ended up signing for her, and later sent her a load of autographed Liverpool team pics for her class.

When I went up to meet the Queen she seemed to have done her homework on football, because she knew I'd been injured and wasn't playing at that moment; she said she hoped I'd be fit again soon.

Darren didn't do so well, unfortunately. He was completely overcome with it all and had to go out a couple of times because he felt sick. The Rolls had gone when we came out, but we managed to get a taxi back to the hotel, and the taxi-driver wouldn't take any money from us – 'My pleasure' – which was nice.

Coincidentally, it was also the night of the Sports Personalities of the Year and Liverpool were getting the team award, so I left London by train and went straight to Anfield to join the team, because they were going to film us live and fit it into the evening presentation programme.

Now they were televising our piece from the directors' guest-room at the ground, but you don't realize what's going on back in the studio, whether they can hear you, or whether they're laughing or whatever. They'd brought some badges out around that time, one of which said, 'Tommy Smith is prettier than Sophia Loren', and Jimmy Hill persuaded me to wear one.

So I was determined to get one over on him, and when we were on the air I said it wasn't so much the Jimmy Hill Show as the Benny Hill Show, which seemed to go down well with everyone except poor Jim. But then he hadn't got much of a chance anyway surrounded by sixteen footballers.

And when I got back Susie said, 'He forgot to mention your MBE,' so I said, 'Well, I'm not really worried. Anyway, it's understandable. He hasn't got one!' You could say it was a full and interesting day.

To my mind, Jimmy Hill is taking the fun out of football, out of having a pint and an argument with your mates in the pub. You could be saying, 'Did you see that penalty? Bloody hell, Casey got whipped up in the box there . . .' and someone else will say, 'Oh no he wasn't. Jimmy Hill showed it in slow-motion and he was a yard outside.' And that's an end to it – there's no answer to that.

So the pub discussion these days is not about Liverpool *v.* Notts Forest or whoever but whether Jimmy Hill was right or wrong in his analysis. It must put the referees under pressure too, knowing the television cameras are on them and that Jimmy Hill is going to analyse their every decision.

Anyway, back to my MBE – I still don't know why I got mine, except that I'd played football a long while. I even tried to put it down to scoring the goal in Rome, but it must have been suggested long before that.

It's still a privilege, and I look on it as an honour for Liverpool to say they took somebody under their wing from Scottie Road and turned him into an award-winning footballer. You could imagine Cally getting an MBE, but then he wasn't the kid from the wrong side of the tracks like me.

When I had to start thinking about not playing football again, it worried me no end. To be truthful, there was nothing else I really wanted to do. Even though I'd been involved in business ventures with my partner George Downey for ten years my heart was still in football.

I wasn't keen to take a manager's job, though there were plenty of offers, because Bill Shankly and Bob Paisley were the only two people I'd known who knew that much about the game they didn't have to worry . . . yet even that didn't stop either of them worrying a lot!

Neither was I keen to go back to the States as a coach. It was good while it lasted but I've seen both sides of the American soccer coin now, and it can be cruel at times.

I really relished getting involved with youngsters again, so I was more than pleased to accept a job back on the Anfield staff – back where I started if you like, helping to look after today's groundstaff lads . . . honestly, they don't know how lucky they are!

I've learnt a lot from the bit of coaching I've done. You don't play eighteen years for the top club in Europe under two bosses and come out with nothing. I don't have to prove anything to anybody. Experience like that speaks for itself.

Football has been good to me, but I also feel I've missed a lot while I've been playing. My kids have grown up very quickly, and they've got used to me not being there. During the last close-season Janette was in bed, half dozing late one night, when I went in to kiss her goodnight.

'Daddy,' she asked, 'will you still be here when I wake up tomorrow. . . ?'

I'd like to catch up a little on what I've missed, on what they've missed too. I suppose you could also say, deep down, that I don't really want to grow up myself. If I could be Peter Pan and live in Never-Never land for the rest of my life I would. The enjoyment I got from being a player is greater than the enjoyment I reckon I'll get from anything else. But then, nobody can stop time running out. . . .